ACTIVITY IN THE PR[...]

Swimming

Activity in the Primary School
General Editor: Don Buckland

Titles in the series
Games and Sports *by W. M. Wise*
Swimming *by David Morris*
Dance *by Peter Lofthouse*
Drama *by Janet Goodridge*
Gymnastics *by Don Buckland*
Reading *by Peter Horner*
Using the Urban Environment *by Michael Williams and Stephen Bell*
Art *by Seymour Jennings*
Music *by Muriel Hart*

Swimming

by
David Morris

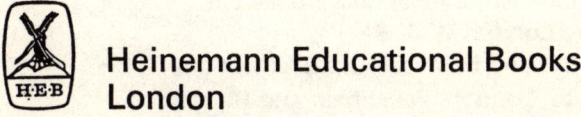
Heinemann Educational Books
London

Heinemann Educational Books Ltd
LONDON EDINBURGH MELBOURNE AUCKLAND TORONTO
HONG KONG SINGAPORE KUALA LUMPUR
IBADAN NAIROBI JOHANNESBURG
LUSAKA NEW DELHI

ISBN 0 435 80600 9

© David Morris 1969
First published 1969
Reprinted with corrections 1974

Published by Heinemann Educational Books Ltd
48 Charles Street, London W1X 8AH
Printed Offset Litho and bound in Great Britain by
Cox & Wyman Ltd, London, Fakenham and Reading

Introduction to the Series

Young children have an instinctive delight in movement. They respond with pleasure to a natural urge to run, jump, throw, climb and dance. The teacher who sets out to develop this energy into useful and creative activities can expect his pupils to be enthusiastic and responsive. The experience is likely to be particularly rewarding for both teacher and class, for during the period of development covered by this series of handbooks, the growth of skill, awareness, versatility and confidence is dramatic. The teacher does not need to be an expert performer or to hold specialist qualifications in physical education. In fact, one hopes that the children in our Infant and Junior Schools will continue to be taught by those who are first and foremost experts in the teaching of children. In Middle Schools a qualified teacher who can serve as the power house for physical education will be needed, although it is to be hoped that he will not adopt the traditional role of the specialist. His task will be to inspire, enthuse, co-ordinate and guide the rest of the staff in their work with their classes, and, by virtue of his own personal ability and example, to set the tempo of the extra-curricular programme.

Moving and Growing drew attention to the ways in which children learn – by repetition, by exploration, through creation, through contact with each other, with the teacher and other adults. How teachers create learning situations according to the nature of each individual child and the stage he has reached. Planning, organization and knowledge are necessary, and this series of handbooks sets out to provide this help. They offer suggestions for work in a balanced programme of physical education for the stages of education suggested by the Plowden Report, i.e. the first eight years of compulsory schooling from five years to twelve plus.

Drama is included in the series, in addition to Games, Gymnastics, Swimming and Dance, because of its obvious links with movement, and its value as an activity whereby so much of the work in the Primary

School may be integrated. It is not suggested that all five aspects of physical education will be covered concurrently. It might be more effective to deal intensively with one or two activities for a concentrated block of time. We do suggest, however, that all aspects should be included in a balanced programme for each stage of primary education.

The tremendous growth of new subjects and new approaches in the Primary School in recent years has made very great demands upon the teacher. Time for planning and preparation is precious, and there is a danger that physical education will either be seen merely as a chance for letting off steam, or will be squeezed out altogether by the pressure of other work. It is hoped that this series will enable the teacher to see the subject as contributing to the process of education as a whole; as another way of assisting the development of children.

Note to 1974 impression

Since this book was written four years ago there have been many changes. We have adopted decimal currency, we are beginning to think metric, costs have risen considerably, many new books on swimming have been written and world swimming records have been broken. Readers of this book are asked to bear these things in mind and to adjust the text of the book where they feel it is necessary. The fundamentals in the book remain the same.

DON BUCKLAND
General Editor

Foreword

My dictionary describes a foreword as 'An opening statement, an explanation as to why the book is written, an opportunity to describe and excuse its defects and the setting forth of the writer's general views on the subject of the book'.

Why has the book been written? The simple answer is that I was invited to write it. With some trepidation, but not realizing what was involved, and, very conscious of the honour bestowed upon me, I agreed. There are already in existence some forty quite recent and all excellent books on swimming written by experts who know far more about the teaching of swimming than I do and who can express themselves far more clearly. My first piece of advice to the reader is to beg, borrow or steal, or even buy, a copy of as many of these books as you can and read them thoroughly. With one exception every one of these books has the word 'swim' or 'swimming' in the title. The title of the exception is *To Start You Crawling* and it was once suggested to me that this was a handbook either for those who were seeking promotion or for very young babies!

The dictionary defines the second point as being an opportunity of describing and excusing its defects. I am most grateful for this opportunity as I am very conscious of the defects which you will find in it. I am no expert and the other twenty thousand qualified teachers of swimming might all make a better job of it than I have. There is very little new in the teaching of swimming which can be written about – there has been a slow process of evolution – and although the presentation of the books on swimming has improved tremendously in recent years most of what is written has been written before in some other form.

The third and last definition of a foreword is that it should set forth the general views of the writer on the subject. I feel that the book itself should do this and this is for you to judge. I believe, as so many of my colleagues do, that it is our job to try to teach every school child to swim. It is not always an easy task, sometimes it does seem impossible, but with the ever-increasing and improving facilities for the teaching of swimming, our job has become a lot easier.

This book is written, as the title suggests, for the teachers in the Primary Schools. Too often in the past, mainly because of the restriction of facilities, swimming has been confined to the children in the top years of the Junior Departments. It is most encouraging to find that more and more infants are being introduced to water and are being taught to swim at an early age. I do hope that all teachers will find something of interest and of value in its pages. Perhaps it should have been called an anthology of bits and pieces about swimming because what is written has been picked up through watching, listening, reading and doing in over thirty years' connection with this, the finest of all sports.

DAVID MORRIS

Contents

1. Mainly Historical — 1

2. Water Space — 6
   (a) Public Facilities — 7
   (b) Future Development — 7
   (c) Teaching Swimming Baths in Schools — 11
   (d) Provision of a Teaching Swimming Bath — 14

3. Why and How — 28
   (a) Why? — 28
   (b) How? — 29

4. The First Time In — 34
   (a) Baths Procedure — 34
   (b) Water Confidence — 35
   (c) Artificial Aids — 36

5. Attainment Tests — 43

6. Having Fun! — 47

7. Artistic Executions — 51
   (a) Methods — 52
   (b) Development of Swimming Strokes — 53
   (c) The Strokes — 56

8. Water Safety — 66

9. Omissions — 69

Appendices
A. List of Addresses — 73
B. Books on Swimming — 75
C. Wall Charts, Pamphlets and Posters — 79
D. Swimming Films, Film Strips and Loops — 80
E. Swimming Awards — 83

Chapter 1: Mainly Historical

Air, and not water, is the natural element of man. Yet man has been swimming since time began. In the early days of history one imagines that there was little time for recreation, life was too much of a struggle for existence and man swam to catch food, to avoid wild beasts and to cross rivers. The earliest forms of artificial aids were fallen tree trunks or blown-up animal skins which supported the 'swimmer' as he held them in front of him when crossing the rivers. I read that Homer in his Iliad, written about 1,000 B.C. says of Hector's charioteer that he fell 'Like a diver diving for oysters'.

There are many variations on the theme of the old proverb, 'Needs must when the devil drives' and necessity has proved to be perhaps the finest of all teachers of swimming. Countless thousands of children who live in the houseboats and river craft in many parts of the world have been able to swim probably before they could walk, otherwise they would not survive. This does not mean that I am an advocate of the practice of throwing children into deep water with the words 'swim or sink'.

'The Baths include an area of more than 20 acres and are fitted with reading rooms, halls, running tracks, covered walks and planted gardens, surrounding the main building which alone covers six acres. In the central buildings the halls are so vast that thousands can wander through them at one time, the rooms have vaulted ceilings 70 feet above the floor and there is an enclosed swimming pool 200 feet long.' This sounds like the brochure description of a new and super 'Crystal Palace' but it is, in fact, a description of a bath built in Rome over 2,000 years ago. At the same time there were six other baths, all equally luxurious, in Rome and, in every province of the Roman Empire, there were similar baths although perhaps not quite as large. These baths were called Tepidaria and were lined with marble, the floors were decorated with mosaics and the walls were surfaced with coloured veined marble. They were heated by furnaces under the floor and as the bather moved towards the section under which the fires were kept the water became warmer and then gradually got cooler as he moved to the other end. The bather then took a final dip in a cold bath so that he would not catch cold when he went outside. On the payment of one cent any Roman citizen could spend the whole day in the bath and its premises, either in the water or listening to discussions, lectures or poetry readings. Those were the days!

No records are available of the strokes used or times taken to cover certain distances, nor was swimming included in the first Olympics of those days so perhaps they swam for pleasure alone! There is also no mention of the fair sex being allowed to participate in these pleasures! As the years have gone by people have learnt to swim faster, for longer times and for farther distances. In August 1875 the whole world was agog with the wonderful achievement of Captain Matthew Webb who swam the English Channel from Dover to Calais in just under twenty-two hours – a phenomenal feat in those days. Fifty-one years later the first woman to conquer the Channel, Gertrude Ederle, swam it in just over seven hours' less time than Captain Webb. Unlike Captain Webb who used the breast stroke, she used the crawl stroke practically all the way.

Swimming the Channel has become so commonplace that it hardly receives a mention in the newspapers. So many people were attempting it that a Channel Swimming Association was formed to regulate the sport and provide observers. There are massed start races and even relay races in which quite young children have taken part. One of the finest achievements was that of Antonio Abertondo of Argentina who made another page of swimming history in 1961 when he swam the Channel both ways with only a five-minute rest. His total time was just over forty-three hours and he was sustained by coffee and chicken soup. As the crow flies the distance he covered was 42 miles but because of cross-currents he actually swam over 80 miles. Previously he had already swum the Channel on three separate occasions, each time from France to England. In 1957 this marathon swimmer performed a colossal feat by swimming 273 miles in the River Parana in Argentina in just under eighty-one hours. Although he swam with the current it was a great achievement to have covered this distance at an average speed of almost 3·4 miles per hour. Another great marathon swimmer was John Sigmund of the U.S.A. who, in 1940, swam for over eighty-nine hours down the Mississippi River and covered 292 miles. It makes one exhausted even to think of these exploits!

Probably a whole book could be written on the evolution of the swimming stroke and it would make fascinating reading. During the latter half of the nineteenth century the main stroke appeared to be the breast stroke, sometimes known as the 'frog' stroke for the movements appear to have been derived from watching a frog in action in the water. Most swimmers used the breast stroke or a form of side stroke, either underarm or overarm, and the latter was quite a popular stroke even during the 'thirties. Although it is not now an 'official' stroke I think it still has its uses and, when no-one is looking I still use it occasionally! The next development was a stroke introduced by a man called Trudgen after whom the stroke was named. In this stroke both arms recovered alternately above the water and a modified form of the scissors kick was developed. It is said that Trudgen saw this stroke being used by natives in South America.

The fastest stroke in the world today is the crawl stroke and its origins are said to lie in the South Sea Islands and many stories are told of its introduction to the world of competitive swimming at the turn of the century. My favourite story, which I believe is based on fact, is very briefly as follows. In 1898 an excited crowd of spectators were at the Bronte Baths in Sydney, Australia watching a curly-headed black-skinned boy threshing his way through the water at such a speed that he made his fellow competitors seem terribly slow. They were all swimming the trudgen stroke but he was swimming the only stroke he knew, the 'tuppa tuppala' – a stroke used for generations by the Solomon Islanders. 'Look at that boy crawling over the water' shouted one of the spectators and so was the Crawl Stroke named. This is the story and who are we to disbelieve such an enchanting tale? The name of the boy was Alec Wickham who was born in the Solomon Islands and had come to live in Sydney. For quite a long time Alec held the world's fifty yards' championship.

The stroke as swum by Alec Wickham appeared to have its limitations for although it was excellent for short distances it was not successful over longer ones. However the Australians took up the crawl stroke and modified the leg action and the introduction of it caused the greatest revolution in swimming style known. Two great Australian swimmers, Barney Keiran and Dick Cavill, discarded their trudgen in favour of it and Dick Cavill introduced it to England when he came to compete in the English Championships in 1902. Using this stroke he later captured the world record for 100 yards in 58 seconds, a remarkable achievement for that time. At one time Cavill had gained 42 National Championships and Keiran, who followed Cavill to England in 1904, used the crawl to set up world records for every distance from 200 yards to one mile. For nearly twenty-five years this stroke kept the Australian swimmers ahead of the world.

Back stroke swimming has always appeared as an inverted form of whatever front stroke happened to be in fashion at the time. At the end of the last century and at the beginning of this one the two methods of swimming on the back were known as the English Back Stroke and the Elementary Back Stroke and these were really inverted forms of the Breast Stroke. The breast stroke type kick on the back is still used particularly for life-saving and survival swimming. Following the advent of the front crawl it was not long before the back crawl, which is fundamentally the same stroke as the front crawl swum on the back, was introduced into competitive swimming and became the second fastest stroke. Since 1912 when it was introduced there have been several refinements in the stroke and to me it is by far the most attractive stroke to watch in competitive swimming.

It was not until the early thirties that there was any further major development in swimming strokes and this development was, of course, the introduction of the butterfly stroke. It is said that one of the most famous breast stroke swimmers of the world, a German, used to fling his arms into the air at the end of each length to give him added impetus to reach the end and turn. Other breast stroke swimmers started to bring their arms out of the water, perhaps two or three times in a length, and found this gave them added speed. This was a very unorthodox form of breast stroke but did not violate any of the laws of breast stroke at that time. Indeed official sanction for its use was given in 1937. The Americans experimented with the leg movement and the dolphin kick was evolved. It was called the butterfly stroke because the flight of the arms through the water bore some resemblance to a butterfly in flight. During the 1952 Olympics this stroke was used by all the men swimmers in the breast stroke races and with great success. A meeting of F.I.N.A. (Federation Internationale Natation Amateur), the world federation controlling swimming, following these Olympics, agreed that breast stroke and butterfly stroke were two quite separate strokes and should be swum as separate events. Many swimmers felt that this stroke would be too exhausting to be taken up seriously, and indeed it does require great stamina and strength, but the same criticism was made about the crawl stroke when that was first introduced. It is interesting to note that it was first introduced, and with some misgivings, into the English Schools' Swimming Association's National Championships in 1953 and the record time then set up for the 100 yards was 68·4 seconds. In 1966 this record was lowered to 57·8 seconds – a decrease of more than 10 seconds in only thirteen years. Now the butterfly stroke is swum by boys and girls of all ages.

Before leaving this brief introduction to the story of swimming some mention must be made of diving. For many years it has been an integral part of all swimming galas although the majority of baths rarely had the facilities for more than plain diving from a low firm board. With the coming of specially-built diving pools and better boards the standard of diving has improved tremendously and, because to be a good diver one does not necessarily have to be a good swimmer, although this is often the case, there is an increasing tendency to separate swimming events from diving events.

Man has dived since history began although most diving would have been done from the surface. Natives have always dived after fish and other inhabitants of the deep and long before the days of artificial appliances were able to stay under water for quite long periods. But diving as we know it today is of comparatively recent origin and is a form of development from the tumbling routines for which the German and Swedish acrobats became so well known. 'Fancy' diving first appeared in the Olympic programme in 1908 but the dives were fairly straightforward bearing little comparison with multiple dives and intricate twists of the divers of today. There have been frequent changes in the composition of the diving tables and great developments have been seen. The increasing use of the trampoline for training has been an important factor in the improvement in the standards of diving, a sport which has become one of the most interesting branches of aquatics.

Chapter 2: Water Space

To be able to learn to swim one must have access to some form of water space whether it be in a river, in the sea or in a swimming bath. Thousands of us learnt to swim in a river or lake, probably without supervision – a menace to ourselves and others – in water probably alive with deadly microbes, and thousands more will probably learn in the same way! In my youth facilities in many areas were almost non-existent and one had to make do with whatever was available. Our local council were generous and allowed us to swim in the lake in the public park with no charge so long as we were away by 8.0 a.m.! Every three or four years the lake was emptied to be cleaned out and it took many weeks and dozens of lorries to remove the slimy mud, the rusty tins, the broken glass, putrefying fish and the occasional dead cat from where we had enjoyed our free swims! This same water supplied the public swimming bath where we were taken for our swimming lessons from school. This bath was maintained by the fill-and-empty method and there was no chlorination or filtration plant! The bath was emptied on Thursday evenings and filled again on Fridays with cold, pale green water from the lake. By the following Thursday you could not see any part of your body which was more than three inches below the surface of the water – and yet nobody was 'lost' as far as I know!

There are still isolated examples of schools overcoming the greatest of difficulties to enable their children to have the opportunity of learning to swim. The pupils of one school in the far North of England travel twenty-three miles each way, once a week in their own time and paying their own fares, to the nearest swimming bath! May I quote an extract from a letter I received from a Headmistress who was determined that her children should be taught to swim. The school, by the way, was in a rural area within three or four miles of the boundary of a large city with a new super swimming bath. The river referred to is the River Thames.

We walk for approximately three-quarters of a mile over swampy ground, across a small stream and carry with us a ladder, a long bamboo pole and a lifebelt. In the river we have erected a safety boom of angle iron and wire netting. Our changing accommodation is composed of sheets of corrugated iron, open to the sky. At the beginning of the season we scoop out the mud which has collected in the boom and cut back thirty yards of nettles, rushes and figwort. We are entirely dependent on the weather.

Yet in spite of these great difficulties some 80 per cent of the leavers were able to swim and four years ago every leaver could swim 100 yards!

These are exceptional cases but they do show us if the will is there what can be done.

(a) Public Facilities

At the beginning of the century the number of indoor swimming baths was very small although in some large cities there was quite good provision. Often this provision was linked with facilities for both the washing of the body and of clothes. Most of these baths were almost identical in design with the high-pitched glass roof. The swimming pool itself was generally 25 yards long, although occasionally $33\frac{1}{3}$ yards, oblong in shape sloping from 3 feet to 6 feet deep and with fixed wooden diving boards. Many of these baths have had a 'face-lift' and have become most attractive. Since the last war there have been quite a number of new baths built and local authorities have vied with each other to build almost palaces as status symbols. Many of these vast new baths have cost anything from one half to a million pounds and will be a burden to the ratepayers for very many years.

(b) Future Development

Unfortunately there has been little national planning in the provision of facilities for swimming. Advisory Councils for Sport and Recreation have been set up in various regions of the country but these Councils must and do take a very long time to become effective. They have to examine the problems in their areas, set up Working Parties, collect information, issue reports etc. and this all takes time. Their purpose is excellent and part of their job is to encourage close consultation between local authorities, to consider the demands of a particular area in relation to the neighbouring areas and to achieve economy by encouraging the joint provision and the joint use of available facilities.

The provision of Olympic standard swimming baths is such a costly business that it is unrealistic to expect every local authority to provide them and yet, because of the arbitrary nature of local boundaries, it would be possible to find identical facilities within a mile or two of each other. I believe that the need for these Olympic standard baths is limited, particularly in such a relatively small country as ours. Perhaps eight of these baths would be sufficient, as long as they were well spaced, to cater for the needs of the very small minority of swimmers who need these special facilities.

With more and more children leaving their schools able to swim each year, with children learning to swim at an earlier age and with so many adults becoming swimmers our whole aim should be to provide better, but not necessarily more extravagant, facilities for swimming within easy access of people's homes. If this was a new country or one where there were no facilities then it would be very easy to plan for the country as a whole. It is still not impossible to work out a plan, taking into account existing facilities. My suggestions for the possible development of a pattern for the provision of swimming facilities would be:

1. *Area Baths*

The whole country would be divided into perhaps seven or eight regions in each of which would be an Area Bath which would be of Olympic standards. Within the region each local and county authority would between them accept responsibility for the cost and upkeep of the area bath. The bath should be situated in a position where there was fairly easy access by public transport and should have, if possible, some overnight accommodation near at hand. The area bath could be used by any competent swimmer and facilities could be provided for the teaching of swimming if this was thought necessary. Properly-equipped diving areas of a high standard would be provided. The main purpose of these baths would be to provide facilities for

  (*a*) Advanced swimming and diving training
  (*b*) County or Inter-County Competitions
  (*c*) National and International Events.

2. *District Baths*

District Baths would be smaller than Area Baths and not as elaborate. They would be the responsibility of a large local authority or a combination of two or more smaller authorities.

These baths would provide good facilities for training, club activities, inter-district events etc.

3. *Neighbourhood Baths*
In every suburb of a large town, in every small town and in each area of population there would be a Neighbourhood Bath. The bath itself need not be longer than 25 yards or its metric equivalent, would be simple in design and would give adequate facilities for family bathing, group swimming and older school children.

4. *School Baths*
Each school, or group of schools on one site, would have its own heated and enclosed teaching swimming bath. This would be available during the day for use of the school but during the evenings and holidays it could be used by youth organizations etc. Although such a bath would be part of the school it should be so situated that it could be isolated for out-of-school activities.

Before leaving the public bath system some reference must be made to the 'management'. Gone are the days when a retired ship's engineer would find a cosy niche for himself in charge of the local baths. No longer have we Baths Superintendents; now they are our Baths Managers. Our present day Baths Managers are highly qualified and skilled and have to be masters of many trades. They have to have a knowledge of engineering in all its branches, they must be analysts and experts on water treatment, they must have a knowledge of swimming and life-saving and also of first aid and they must be good public relations men. It is this latter aspect which is so important these days for they have large staffs to manage, they are in close contact with a large and changing public and with schools, and they have to keep their Baths Committee happy! This is not always the easiest of jobs because some elected members feel that swimming baths are a recreational luxury and should be made to pay by cutting the expenses in every possible way and they expect the Baths Manager to run a complex organization with an inadequate and ill-equipped staff. The Baths Manager is often blamed for certain actions which he has had to take to implement the policy and decisions of his Committee. The majority of Baths Managers now work in very close co-operation with the

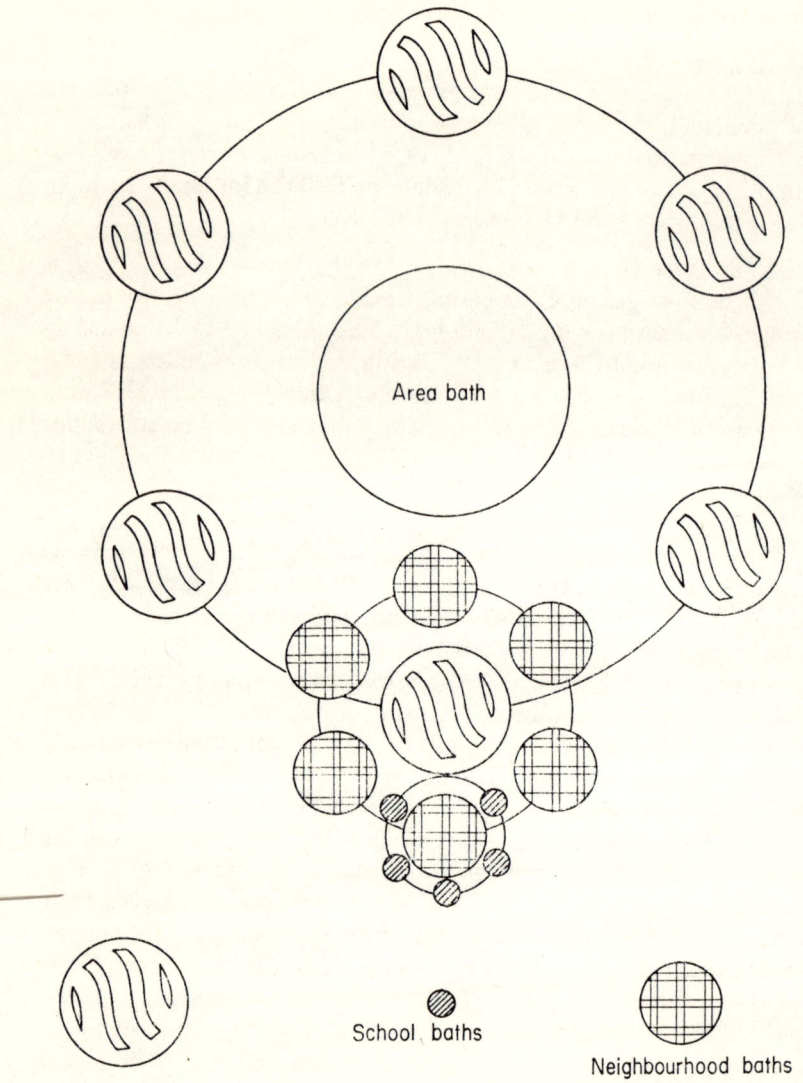

schools and can be a tremendous help in many ways. Even their antipathy to the 'dirty little school pools' has been overcome and they are always most willing to advise and help in the problems which arise.

(c) Teaching Swimming Baths in Schools

For very many years the teaching of swimming in Primary Schools was almost impossible in very many parts of the country because of the lack of facilities. Even where there were baths it often meant a long journey by public transport and a great waste of time and energy. Those Headteachers who were enlightened enough to appreciate the great value of this teaching and allowed some of their children almost a whole school session to give half-an-hour in the baths deserve our commendation. Very often, too, the schools had to share the baths with the general public, and a crowded shallow end in very noisy conditions was not ideal for teaching children water confidence and their early strokes. The introduction of special teaching pools into many baths has been a great help for those schools within easy access but comparatively very few schools are near enough to benefit.

Some twelve years ago the English Schools' Swimming Association launched its 'Teaching Swimming Bath' Scheme and many hundreds of schools and thousands of children must owe their sincere gratitude to the Association but particularly to its founder, Mr Frank Rudge who was so ably supported by the Hon. Treasurer, Mr Harry Cushing. The phenomenal growth in the number of school pools during these last twelve years is almost unbelievable. No accurate figures are available but it is estimated that the number of baths in our Primary Schools was less than 30 at the beginning of this period. Now the figure stands at over 6,000 – a number which is growing all the time quite rapidly. This means that almost 29 per cent of our Primary Schools have their own teaching baths and nearly one million children have the opportunity of learning to swim as part of their normal work in school. A large number of these pools originated through the inspiration of the Teaching Bath Scheme, the advice so freely given and the very many initial interest-free loans given to Headteachers. Tribute must be paid also to the thousands of parents, teachers and friends of the schools who have worked so hard either building the pools themselves or raising the money to pay for contractors to do the work.

The attitude of the Education Authorities has changed tremendously. At the beginning they were rather suspicious, probably rightly so, because they had no idea what was involved and what their responsibilities would be. I think that many of them felt that they would be 'landed' with great big holes in the ground or half-finished concrete boxes which would be of little use and a danger to the children. In the early days when a school put forward its ideas it took many months for a proposed scheme to go through the many departments and committees, and the groups of teachers and parents became very frustrated because they could not make a start although the money and labour force were ready and waiting. Having seen some of these baths completed the authorities began to appreciate what a tremendous asset a teaching swimming bath could be to a school. The children were learning to swim in familiar surroundings during their normal P.E. lesson time, there was no waste of valuable time in travelling, and conditions were ideal. It also meant that far more time would be available at the public baths for those who were not fortunate enough to possess their own baths.

Many authorities either delegated one person to be responsible for swimming baths or appointed a small group of perhaps four or five with representatives from the Education, Health, Architects and Engineers Departments who examined the plans, the site, etc. and who had power to make a decision without further reference to any Committee. Many authorities decided to make a financial contribution to the initial cost and this varied from authority to authority – some gave a percentage grant, others agreed to provide all the chlorination and filtration equipment and others gave a lump sum. The majority agreed to be responsible for full maintenance once the job was completed and approved, but there were one or two exceptions. There are now quite a number of enlightened authorities who have promised that within a very limited time every one of their Primary Schools will have its own teaching bath. This is indeed progress.

Too many authorities believe that one should build for posterity and not to cater for urgent and immediate needs. It was felt that all school pools should be built of reinforced concrete and nothing else was acceptable. Some of our older colleagues will remember temporary swimming pools made on troopships by using a tarpaulin rigged up on to timber supports or part of the deck which proved most effective.

It was felt that something of this sort, a little more elaborate perhaps, would help to supply the great need for water space. Some contractors felt the same way and began to design a simple pool which consisted of a frame in which was suspended a P.V.C. bag although little was known of the durability of the liner or how the whole thing would stand up to our winters. One contractor, who had been a farmer, says that his inspiration came from the success he had had with his own children when he had used a tarpaulin hung from hurdles as a pool on his farm! Many experiments were carried out using timber, metal, concrete slabs and wire netting for the various frames. They were all quite successful and two or three firms went into production. But for a long time Education Committees were not convinced that this type of pool would be satisfactory in a school although the price must have been very tempting. However, eventually one or two authorities allowed them to be tried out and very soon nearly all authorities permitted them to be used, indeed several advocated their use because of their cost, the variety of size available and although permanent enough in construction they could be moved if it was found necessary.

At the same time as this growth in the number of pools in schools there was a parallel and even more rapid growth in the number of pools in private gardens. The number of contractors who were willing to build pools increased almost as rapidly, some of them just wanting to jump on the band wagon and make as much money as they could as quickly as they could. Several schools were to suffer because of the incomplete and poor workmanship of some of these firms who had sprung up almost overnight. Through the auspices of the Teaching Swimming Bath Scheme of the E.S.S.A. a meeting, addressed by Lord Mancroft, one of the Patrons of the Scheme, was called of representatives of firms specially interested in the construction, maintenance and supply of swimming pools and ancillary equipment. As a result of the interest shown in this meeting the Association of Swimming Pool Contractors Ltd. (A.S.P.C.) was formed and 'consumers' can rely on the integrity of its members. They have set standards, and they are high standards, for many aspects such as design, construction, filtration, heating and paints of swimming pool work and these standards are available in printed form to anyone interested.

(d) Provision of a Teaching Swimming Bath

Although there are some 6,000 schools with their own pools now, there are still over 15,000 schools without. Many of these schools are within easy access of excellent facilities at public baths, but there are still very many schools without any opportunity at all of being able to teach their children to swim. It is to these schools that the next few paragraphs are addressed.

I believe that any water space, however small, is better than none and the provision of such a water space is within the capabilities of any school. The problem is most acute in the rural areas where lies the greatest need and it is these schools which are, because of their position, the smallest. But a small pool which could cater for a limited number of children can be obtained for just over £100. This would consist of a box or tank which would contain water and would lack the refinements which help to make life much easier but these refinements could be added later when circumstances permit. I will try to deal briefly with the steps which have to be taken for the provision of a teaching swimming bath.

1. *Raising the Money*

Once the staff of a school have decided that it would be a good idea to have a school pool then the co-operation of the parents must be sought. Without their help and participation, unless one works for one of the exceptional and generous authorities, it will be almost impossible to raise the money which is so necessary to provide any pool. However keen the children themselves are, without their parents' support little can be done. Before calling a meeting with the parents one should approach the local education authority to find out if they agree in principle and also to find out what financial aid would be forthcoming.

Having gained the support and interest of the parents it is suggested that two committees be formed, a technical committee and a finance committee. As the needs and conditions of every school vary so much it is difficult to generalize and it is for the technical committee to examine the possibilities of the particular school. They have to decide (*a*) whether it would be possible to build it themselves, do part of the work or put out the whole job to contractors and (*b*) what type of pool e.g. concrete, free-standing etc. they would like and could afford. Most contractors are very helpful and will give quotations and also advice, and will make allowances for any preparatory work done. Most head-teachers who already have pools would be very willing to allow groups of interested people to see their swimming baths and to give the benefit of their experience.

Having decided on the type of pool to be provided plans have to be drawn up and submitted to the education authority and to the local council from whom planning permission must be received. Consideration must also be given to the means of draining the water from the pool which can be done into the main drainage, into an open ditch in a neighbouring field or by soakaways, and again permission must be sought. Do make early application for planning permission for nothing is more frustrating than having the money and labour force available and then having to wait for weeks and even months for the necessary permission. Do aim also to get the pool completed as soon as possible after the scheme is launched whilst enthusiasm is still keen and parents feel that their own children in the school will benefit. Quite recently I read a report of a pool having been completed in ten years – I think the record is twenty-five years! At the same time as the technical committee have been investigating the types and costs of pools, the finance committee will be meeting to discuss ways and means of raising money.

What appears at first to be a formidable task of raising anything from a couple of hundred to a couple of thousand pounds in a small school is often much easier than it seems provided that the support of the parents is there, for most of the money will come, in the main, from them or their children or friends. Most of you will know the usual round of garden fêtes, jumble sales, autumn fayres (it must be spelt this way!) etc. but the following ideas, which have proved successful elsewhere, may help you.

(a) Find out to what extent the l.e.a. is prepared to help.
(b) Approach the Teaching Swimming Bath Scheme of the E.S.S.A. (address in Appendix A). When they have the money returned from other schools they are prepared to lend up to £300 interest free for three years to the Headteacher. It is surprising what an incentive even the promise of a loan is, and several schools who have asked for such a loan find that they do not require it. Hundreds of schools have been helped already.

(c) Bank Managers are still approachable and can help although they have limitations imposed upon them!

(d) A scheme, which has worked quite well in several schools, whereby a Company is 'floated' and the shares are purchased by the parents and friends. The cost of floating such a company is about £50. If the school require say £2,000 and knows that each year they can raise perhaps £400, then shares up to the value of £2,000 are sold and interest is given. At the end of each year £400 of shares are redeemed by lot. If parents have to leave the district or withdraw their money for any domestic reason then this can be done. At the end of the five years the Company is 'sunk' (I'm sure that is not the right word but it is the opposite of 'floated'). Everybody who invested money gets it back with one to five years of interest and the school has had its pool five years longer than it might have done.

(e) Promises are given by parents to subscribe x shillings per week or per month or one donation towards the costs.

(f) Children in the school are invited to take an 'earn-a-swim' card which can be produced on a duplicating machine or printed. This card can bear the Headteacher's signature and on it are recorded small jobs which the children do for friends and neighbours and for which they receive the odd coppers. The signature of the patron with the amount given is also recorded. I am a firm believer in letting the children be involved and even if the total collected in this way is small they feel that they have done something towards their own pool.

(g) Although everybody does not believe in 'Derby Draws' they are a valuable source of income. But do not forget to register with your local council as a 'Charity' – it only costs a guinea a year and makes you 'legal'.

(h) One school of which I have heard and which was situated in an industrial area ran its own football pool. It was run by the parents (the school itself could not be involved) and the tickets were sold weekly in the local factories and the homes. In twelve months they had paid a contractor to erect a pool and at the end of two years the pool was covered and paid for!

(i) In many districts there are very ancient charities from which money is rarely paid out and the capital continues to grow each year. The terms of some of these charities may allow a grant to be made for the building of a pool – I know of three very fine pools complete with dressing rooms which have been provided for in this way. There is a register of such charities somewhere, probably in the local or county council offices and it is worth investigating.

(j) Sponsored walks are very much in the news these days. In one school the children, the staff and the parents took part and raised quite a large sum with good publicity. What about a sponsored swim at the nearest baths? A local swimming club might help.

(k) An approach to a local firm for a donation often brings results. So does an appeal to a well-known personality who might live in the neighbourhood.

(l) The local Rotary Club or Round Table are most helpful. One Round Table raised sufficient funds to provide three local schools with a swimming pool each. The Inner Wheel, the ladies' section of Rotary, opened a shop in one town to sell bric-à-brac in aid of the local school's swimming pool fund.

(m) Permission was received for collections at a Stock Car Meeting, a Cricket Match, a Football Match, a Wrestling Match and at a Horse Show.

(n) Paving stones round the pool with the initials of the purchaser inscribed have been sold – this could be extended to having your footprint preserved in concrete for posterity!

(o) Apart from Bingo evenings there are many group activities such as Beetle Drives, Wine and Cheese Parties, Musical Evenings, Car Rallies, Flower, Fruit & Vegetable Shows, Fashion Shows, Variety Shows, Pet Shows, Concerts, Square Dances and Dog Shows. In one district the Mayor's Ball was run in aid of the local school's swimming pool.

(p) In several schools a swimming pool has been built by contributions donated as a memorial of a famous 'old boy' of the school.

(q) The passengers on a P. & O. liner, through competitions on board and by donations, raised over £500 towards a swimming pool for the children in a Physically Handicapped School.

(r) Children love collecting things and for a worthy cause they become even more keen. Most things have a sale value particularly if you can find a potential and anxious buyer! So why not have Collection Days for Waste Paper, Stamps, Wool, Bottles, Toys, Comics, Non-ferrous Metal, White Elephants, Handkerchiefs, etc.

(s) If you are on good terms with the manager or owner of the 'local' perhaps you could get him to let you have a 'tower of pennies'. Perhaps you could make a collecting box in the shape of a model of your swimming bath.

(t) Have you tried investing a shilling or two in each child and asking them to invest it in a scheme of their own to find out after three months which child has made it grow the most with a prize perhaps for the winner? You would be amazed at the ingenuity of children! There was the little girl who was keen on making sweets and was very good at it. The first time she was able to make six ounces of sweets with a 50 per cent profit and she went on ploughing back her profits into her capital until she finally made nearly three pounds. There was the boy who bought a white mouse and crossed it with a field mouse and the boy who bought a pair of stick insects – but these are long tales!

I could go on and complete the alphabet but I think that there are sufficient ideas for most finance committees to think about and with a little luck and a lot of co-operation the school could have its pool in 12 months. Three items of interest from our reports – one village school with just 100 children raised £1,600 in 9 months, a bigger Junior Mixed and Infants School raised £5,500 in 21 months and one Primary School are now saving for their second pool (although they do not say what for!).

2. Planning the Bath

(a) Decide that the provision of the bath shall be a short-term project which shall be dealt with in stages as circumstances permit.

Stage 1. Provide a water space i.e. a tank either below or above ground which will hold water. Initially it would mean that the bath would be hand-chlorinated (quite effective and still done in many pools where the public are admitted) and would have to be emptied and refilled possibly every ten days – perhaps a nuisance but well worth the labour involved.

Stage 2. Provide filtration and chlorination plant. The pipework for this should have been provided in Stage 1.

Stage 3. Provide a means of heating the water. This would increase the time when the pool could be used by at least two months per

annum. Warm water is of great advantage when teaching anyone to swim as it helps to remove tension and brings relaxation.
Stage 4. Provide wind barriers or a house to enclose the pool. This may take several years but it is worth bearing in mind.

(b) *Type of pool*
There are two main types, concrete traditional pools and portable 'free-standing' pools. In the main these are rectangular in shape but there are round ones, T-shaped and L-shaped ones and there was one 'caterpillar' pool – a series of arcs for added strength!
(i) *Concrete pools.* These are really rectangular holes in the ground with the sides and base lined with reinforced concrete. These may be deck-level pools i.e. the top of the pool on the same level as the surround but this does encourage dust and dirt falling into the pool. We suggest that the sides of the pool should be from 12 to 18 inches above the level of the surround with a capping 9 to 12 inches wide. This is so much easier for teaching and also keeps the bath water very much cleaner. These may be constructed by one of three methods: (a) The traditional method with reinforced concrete walls and base; (b) By the 'Gunite' process where the hole is lined with wire mesh and liquid concrete is sprayed on to it under great pressure. This has many advantages as layers may be sprayed on to any thickness, there are no joins in the concrete, it is a very quick process taking less than two days and the pool can be constructed on a site difficult of access e.g. an enclosed quadrangle or in a classroom, as the pipes used for the spraying process can be passed through windows or across corridors. This is, of course, a specialized process and only certain firms have the necessary equipment; (c) By using pre-cast hollow concrete blocks with steel rod reinforcement.
(ii) *Free-standing pools.* These pools consist of a frame, generally of treated timber with reinforcing steel bars but there are some with concrete or steel walls, which supports a heavy P.V.C. bag. These have several advantages over the concrete pool; they are a lot cheaper; there is little site preparation; there is less loss of heat in the water; they have many advantages for teaching (although the teacher may get a lot wetter!); there is little danger of a small child or animal accidentally falling into one. The P.V.C. liner has a limited life possibly five or six years but the replacement is not

expensive, possibly about £50. Should the occasion arise they can be moved and they can be added to and made longer or wider and the sides can be either 3 or 4 feet high.

(c) *Size of pool*

As the pool is fundamentally a 'teaching' pool it must be shallow enough for the smallest child to have the utmost confidence and yet be deep enough in which to swim. It is suggested that the depth of water should be about 2' 9" and it is much better if the bath is the same depth all over so that there is no deep end, although a fall of an inch or two may be necessary for drainage purposes. The maximum length should be 50 feet and the width from 20 to 24 feet. Some people suggest that the pool should slope from perhaps 6 inches to 3 feet, but once the children have their feet off the bottom this type of pool has great limitations.

(d) *Site of pool*

Consultation must take place at a very early stage with the education and architects' departments over the siting of the pool because there is always the possibility of the future development of the school site. The site must be firm with no likelihood of an upward rise of water from springs etc. when the pool is completed. Unless dressing rooms and toilets are to be installed, the pool should be readily available to the facilities of the school. There should be easy access to the power supply for the extension of heavy cable can be a very costly item. Consideration should also be given to the distance from main drainage if it is to be used. However well-protected a pool may be it is advisable to site it well away from footpaths and public open spaces. Although not essential, it is better if the pool has a southern aspect. Finally, avoid trees and shadows and, if possible, extraneous noises.

(e) *Drainage of the pool*

The pool is normally drained into the main drainage and for this permission must be sought from the local responsible authority. Even when the pool has a filtration plant and has to be emptied only once a year, back-washing, with a loss of several hundreds of gallons of water, has to take place almost weekly.

Where the soil is suitable, soakaways can be used. It is suggested that three or four of these should be constructed close to each other and connected together so that as the water fills one it can overflow into the next and so on, thus enabling the water to get away more quickly. Where the soil is not suitable for a soakaway and it is not convenient to use main drainage then the water can be run into an open ditch in an adjoining field but the consent of the owner must be sought and it might be wiser to drain only some of the water in the pool at one time.

(f) *The filtration and chlorination of the pool*

The filtration of water means the extraction of the insoluble solids by mechanical means. The water passes through the filter media which extracts the suspended particles. The filter media may be either sand of a special sort and different gradings or diatomaceous earth. Most filters are cleaned by back-washing which is a simple process whereby the flow of water is reversed and flushes the media and the dirty water then runs to waste. This is a process which takes only a few minutes and the frequency when it has to be done depends on the condition of the water and the use of the pool – perhaps once in every five or six days. Most filters have in the system a strainer box which catches larger solids such as leaves and materials.

(i) *Sand filters.* The sand filter consists of a tank which contains some four or five different grades of sands with the larger grades at the bottom. These tanks are generally quite large, some three feet in diameter and four to six feet high. Once the tank is filled, and if properly looked after, it does not have to be emptied and refilled for many years although the top has to be cleaned occasionally. Sand filters are initially more expensive and can cost over £300. They are used by the majority of public baths but once installed they are much easier to maintain.

(ii) *Diatomaceous earth filters.* Diatoms are microscopic marine or freshwater organisms and the 'earth' is composed of the skeletons of millions of these diatoms – it looks like a white powder and is an excellent filter medium. The diatomaceous earth is contained in various types of holders through which the water passes. They are very efficient but the 'earth' does need changing occasionally and they do require some little skill to operate. They are cheaper than sand filters costing from about £150 to £400 depending on the size.

(iii) *Gravity filters.* This is a fairly recent type of filter and is particularly suitable for free-standing pools. The water passes out from the pool, generally through a surface skimmer, into the gravity filter where larger solids are trapped in a removable tray. Beneath this is a foam filter which extracts most of the dirt, and the finer particles are collected in cartridges of filter materials which are easily removed and replaced with new ones. The running costs are low and the filter itself costs in the region of £100. Many local authorities are adopting or authorizing this type of filter in their school pools.

(iv) *Chlorination.* The chlorination of a pool means the adding of sufficient chlorine to the water to kill any bacteria. For school pools the chlorine is generally supplied in liquid form which can be poured into the pool from a can but this hand-chlorination means that there can be pockets of unchlorinated and over-chlorinated water. A very simple form of automatic chlorination is available and this consists of a screw tap with a drip-feed tube with piping to connect the chlorine container to the suction side of the pump. Electric chlorinators are also available and these cost between £30 and £40.

To test the chlorine content of the water there are various test kits on the market and these cost anything from £2 10s 0d. to £10. These kits are also used to test the pH content of the water by comparing a sample of the water to which a reagent has been added with a colour standard.

(g) Heating the pool

The third stage in the planning of the pool is the provision of some form of heating. It is not essential, but if children are to be really receptive at the beginning to water confidence and later to instruction, then it should be heated. When one considers the capital which has been invested in the swimming pool then it is sound economy to extend the season when this can be done by heating the water, particularly in a climate which is as uncertain as ours.

To help to retain the temperature of the water there are many types of floating covers on the market made from a variety of materials. These are put on when the pool is not in use and it is found that by using them overnight the heat loss is reduced to only two or three degrees. These covers also help to prevent debris and leaves falling into the pool. Most of them are fairly easy to manipulate and provision is made for the rain water to get through into the pool, otherwise it would strain the material and the weight would make the removal of the cover a heavy task. This is the big disadvantage of using tarpaulins. For certain types of covers a roller, either fixed or movable, can be fitted at the end of the bath and the cover can be taken off in seconds. The use of these insulating covers reduces the cost of heating almost by half.

There are various means of heating the pool water all of which have some merit but again local conditions must be the deciding factor.

(i) *Electricity*. This is probably the simplest method of heating the water and once installed electric heaters require practically no attention or maintenance. Although not the cheapest form of heating it is probably the most convenient. Generally a time clock is fitted into the heater and the power is automatically switched on when electricity is at its cheapest rate. A thermostat then regulates the temperature. The provision of lengthy service mains is quite an expensive business and one must make certain that the cable at the point of connection is heavy enough to carry the heater load. This load will vary from 12KW for a pool of about 9,000 gallons to 60KW for 48,000 gallons. The price of the provision and installation of a heater will vary from £120 to £300 depending on the size.

(ii) *Gas or Calor Gas*. Gas is an efficient method of heating the water and the cost of heater and installation is a little higher than that of electricity. The temperature of the water can be regulated by a thermostat. There is occasional maintenance and cleaning required. Calor gas is very useful where no other form of heating is available but it does cost nearly twice as much as piped gas.

(iii) *Oil*. Although oil heating is the cheapest, the initial cost of installation is very much higher. Storage tanks have to be built and there is more maintenance of plant.

(iv) *School heaters*. The dual use of school heaters has been quite a success in several schools where the bath was situated fairly near the school boiler house. During the summer months the school heating system would have to be by-passed. This method obviates the purchase and housing of a heating plant, and where the school heating is automatic does not involve much additional labour. It would mean, however, that the school boiler would be in almost continuous use throughout the year, which possibly would not be welcomed by the heating engineers and maintenance men. There must be consultation with the authority's engineers to find out if it is practical and advisable.

(v) *Solar heating.* Although one might feel that we do not get sufficient sun in this country to be able to use solar heating, there are many advocates of it. Indeed a whole school has been heated most efficiently by it. The pool water is pumped so that it trickles between two surfaces of metal or some other material which are heated by the sun and then it is returned to the pool. I have seen this done as an experiment and the water coming out has been almost boiling. The plant is very simple and, once installed, the running costs are almost nil. Experiments are being carried out to find more efficient and even simpler forms of solar heater.

(vi) *Running costs.* Most education authorities undertake to maintain the school bath when it is completed. The maintenance includes the cost of heating but often there are restrictions when the heating may be used. It is difficult to give the actual costs of heating as prices vary quite a lot in different parts of the country and these costs are rising all the time. Of the three main methods of heating, oil, gas and electricity, it will be found that oil is the cheapest and electricity the most expensive, but there is not a great deal of difference.

As a very rough guide to the costs of heating the following will give you some idea. To raise the temperature of 10,000 gallons of water by one degree Fahrenheit:

 Oil   = $\frac{7}{8}$ of the cost of a gallon of oil
 Gas   = $1\frac{1}{4}$ times the cost of a therm of gas
 Electricity = 30 times the cost of an off-peak unit of electricity.

(h) *Covering the pool*

Very many primary schools would like to cover their swimming pools with some form of 'sun-house' but are prevented from doing so by the quite high cost of these enclosures which cost more than the complete pool itself. Others feel that the season from the beginning of May until mid-October is long enough and that it is a good thing to have a rest during the winter months. Again so much will depend on local circumstances and facilities already provided in the school.

If money was unlimited then one could follow the example of the City of Liverpool which has provided at least twelve of its schools with a 'packaged-deal' pool, costing from £10,000 to £25,000, enclosed in a most attractive building, well-designed, containing all the plant, including heating, and dressing rooms, toilets and showers. If one is prepared to build the enclosure oneself it probably could be done for between £700 and £800. For such a building one could use the steel structure of a barn as a basis and clad it with some form of P.V.C. sheeting or fibreglass.

One firm is advertising an enclosure with a material called 'Sintilon' which covers a galvanized steel or concrete framework from ground level to ground level. This costs about £1,700. It is claimed by the makers that with such an enclosure one can have eight months' full use of the pool without heating and all-the-year swimming with low cost space heating.

Another firm makes an enclosure of aluminium construction with translucent fibreglass cladding. There are closable ventilation flaps on the long sides and there are sliding doors at each end. The whole structure is corrosion resistant and therefore the maintenance is almost nil. One may have to build a small wall to support the structure and this can cost several hundred pounds. The cost of such an enclosure to cover a pool 50' by 15' with a 4' surround is approximately £2,300.

A new technique using reinforced polyester as the structural material for a cover has been very successful. The structure is described as 'consisting of interacting hyperbolic paraboloid units bolted together and to concrete foundations only 2 feet deep'. The whole structure is unsupported and has a modern and pleasing appearance. Its advantages are lightness, ease of transport and erection and weatherability and it is claimed that it is some 25 per cent cheaper than any other comparable structure.

A firm which has pioneered Space Structures in this country and abroad are developing one for covering small pools. They use barrel vaults covered in translucent sheet for spans up to 32 feet with no limit on length. They use throughout aluminium alloy and fibre glass or other similar sheet as these materials are highly corrosion resistant and do not suffer the problems which are found with steel or reinforced concrete when the atmosphere is affected by chlorinated water.

One of the latest developments or experiments is called a Russian Pool Shelter which has many attractive features. I am told that it originates from an idea which is used in Russia to quite a large extent. It is a form of windbreak which is used in conjunction with a heated bath. It is a simple wall with a roof which covers 6 feet of the surround of the pool and leaves the space above the pool open. The walls consist of a 1" tubular steel frame with treated plywood panels to a height of 3' 6" above which is translucent sheeting. The roof is covered with the same sheeting. Warm air can be ducted or blown round the sides and over the pool which raises the air temperature and permits instruction with comfort and extends quite considerably the swimming season. One of the major drawbacks of a complete enclosure, condensation, is non-existent. The whole shelter can be supplied as a 'do-it-yourself' kit and can be erected by unskilled people and the total cost is just over £500.

It will be seen from the few examples I have referred to above that contractors appreciate that there is a big demand for small pool enclosures and that they are making a great effort to meet this demand with good quality yet reasonable structures.

Conclusion

In conclusion, brief reference should be made to what is to me a most encouraging trend. I refer to the increasing number of infants who are being taught to swim not only in the pools of the primary schools of which they form part but in pools which have been built in infant schools. I believe that the earlier a child has the opportunity of learning to swim the easier it is to teach the child. With the advent of 'First' and 'Middle' Schools and the re-organizing of the present primary schools many school baths will, by their location, become the property of one of the new schools and many children may lose the opportunities they have enjoyed. We may, therefore, find an increased demand for new school baths which perhaps would be more specifically designed for First or Middle Schools. This may be looking ahead for many years.

In the meantime how do primary schools cater for their five-year-olds as well as for their older juniors? Many schools feel, as I do, that it is better to introduce the younger infants to swimming by using shallower water, possibly not more than 2 feet deep. This means that the pool is part emptied for perhaps one day a week with the resultant loss of several hundreds of gallons of warm water. Then it has to be refilled again with cold water which will take some time to heat up to the required temperature. What I should like to see, and I am surprised that no swimming pool contractor has suggested it as yet, is the provision of a small tank, perhaps ten or twelve feet square and two feet deep, which is adjacent to the school pool. When the school pool depth of water has to be lowered the surplus water would be fed into this tank through the circulation system. Not only would this save the water, which would be pumped back again into the main pool, but it would give an additional teaching space for the younger or more nervous children. An additional small pump might have to be installed. The whole of this addition could be provided at a very reasonable cost.

I offer my apologies for the length of this chapter. What is written is probably common knowledge to so many of you. On the other hand there are still hundreds of schools without any facilities for the teaching of swimming and if it has helped only a few of them then it has been worthwhile. Without water space there can be no swimming.

Chapter 3: Why and How

Why?
Why teach swimming? Should swimming be included in the already very full curriculum of the Primary School?

To answer the second question first the answer is a very definite 'yes'. This answer will be justified in the reasons I give to the question 'Why teach swimming?'. As long ago as 1914 the Amateur Swimming Association, which had done such a lot to encourage the teaching of swimming, joined with the National Union of Teachers in sending a deputation to the Board of Education. The deputation met with the success it deserved for the Minister of Education agreed that in future swimming should become part of the curriculum of the schools of the country. This was a great achievement for, although there had been some teaching of swimming in schools – probably unofficial – prior to that date, from then on we find that the teaching of swimming in our schools has grown continuously, a growth which was limited only by the lack of facilities. Because of the ever-increasing facilities provided by the introduction of Teaching Swimming Baths during the last twelve years this growth has been almost phenomenal.

Swimming is fun! It is more fun than any other sport. It is one of the most popular, the cheapest and the best of all sports. It can be enjoyed by both young and old – indeed at almost any time from 'the cradle to the grave'. It is not a sport for the select few for almost everyone can join in and it is the ideal family sport. It can be enjoyed on one's own or with friends and, on a competitive basis, as an individual or as part of a team. To achieve moderate success one does not have to have great strength or techniques. One can take part in swimming and derive great pleasure from it right through life far beyond the time when one has to give up most other sports. There is a healthy pleasure in swimming and with this pleasure goes a certain challenge and perhaps a feeling of adventure. Although man is a dry land animal he can learn to enjoy water by knowing how to swim.

The therapeutic values of swimming have long been recognized and many of our large hospitals have their own swimming pools where the rehabilitation of patients is encouraged after serious illness or injury. For the physically handicapped and the disabled, swimming is the one sport where they become on almost equal terms with their more fortunate colleagues.

Although most lessons should be enjoyable, we cannot include in the timetable all those things which are fun and give us pleasure for these reasons alone. These are the reasons why I think that the teaching of swimming should be a part of the physical education of the child and should be included in the timetable of every school.

1. The ability to swim gives the child a skill which ensures that he will be able to survive in water for as long a time as possible.

2. A competent swimmer can, in an emergency, not only save his own life but that of another provided that he has had proper training in life-saving.

3. Swimming is an ideal exercise for all-round development unequalled in any other form of sport.

4. Not only does swimming contribute to the physical development of the child but it increases physical skill and gives a constant sense of achievement.

5. Swimming helps to develop mental and physical co-ordination, self-control and confidence.

6. It builds character and encourages perseverance and, for the more able who wish to take part in competitive swimming, determination, self-discipline and dedication.

7. It helps to equip the child to enjoy to the full and with safety the increasing number of water sports, such as canoeing, rowing, sailing, water-ski-ing and sub-aqua swimming, all sports which should be open only to those who are competent swimmers.

8. Being unable to swim one misses one of life's great pleasures and one may get a sense of frustration and a feeling of inferiority. This latter feeling is why it is always so much more difficult to teach a teenager or adult than a young child.

How?

There is no best method of teaching swimming. Every teacher is as much an individual as every child and what suits one may not be the most suitable method for another. There are general principles which can be suggested but it is up to the individual to interpret these to suit himself and to suit the children who are being taught.

Our aim should be to help each child to attain the maximum development possible for that child. No two children are alike. They vary in age, size, strength, intelligence, endurance and, in what is very important, natural ability. All these factors determine the time in which it takes to teach a child to swim. Some children can be taught to 'swim' (here I mean the ability to get the feet off the bottom of the bath and progressing through the water a short distance) in their first lesson – others may take weeks or months very often because of an inbred fear of the water. It is quite normal for one's first reaction to water to be fear for it is air and not water which is man's natural element.

A teacher does not have to be a good swimmer to be a good teacher of swimming although it does help to be able to show the children on rare occasions how to do some particular thing. It does no harm for the children to see that what 'sir' says ought to be done can be done and that the teacher is not just a theorist! I do say 'rare occasions' because I believe that if the children are in the water, the teacher should be out of it. It is difficult enough to watch all the children when you are at the bathside – it is impossible to do it when you are in the water. The one exception I would make is when the children are very young or perhaps going into the bath for the first time and the presence of the teacher very close to them will give them that extra bit of confidence they might need, but there should always be another responsible person present.

The teacher in charge of the class has the full responsibility of the class not only for its conduct but for the safety of every child. Therefore every teacher of swimming should have an elementary knowledge of life-saving and resuscitation. It may never happen but one must be prepared!

It is said that a good teacher can teach under any conditions however poor, but such a teacher would be a far better teacher under ideal conditions. Those with pools in their schools or with access to the specially designed teaching pools are very fortunate because the pool becomes your classroom and you are in charge. Many of you will have experienced the difficulties which arise when you are trying to teach children in a public bath when the public are allowed in at the same time, particularly when a neighbouring school has a holiday in honour of a certain Saint or for what used to be known as a 'teachers' rest' day! You may, too, have shared my experience of telling off some particularly inattentive child only to find that he does not belong to the school at all – they do all look rather alike in the water!

To get the best results from the children they should be happy and relaxed and they can only be relaxed if the water is warm enough. If you have some control of the temperature of the bath then you should aim to raise the temperature to at least 70°F, particularly for beginners. It is always very noticeable that when the air temperature is lower, then the water temperature seems so much higher.

In the initial stages of teaching swimming keep the lessons short. It is far better for the children to come out of the pool wanting more. Never force a child to do anything. Seeing the other children practising will often encourage a nervous child to try to follow their example. In the early stages all movements in the water should be performed fairly slowly – accidental mouthfuls have a most unnerving effect on most learners. Gentleness and patience must be used to overcome the natural fears which some children suffer. The greatest advantage of the free-standing pool is that the teacher is on the same level as the children and does not have to shout to make himself heard but can talk to them in ordinary conversational tones. The very proximity of the teacher does give confidence although one can get very wet in the process!

So do try to dress for the part in appropriate costume. I have seen teachers trying to teach swimming in their overcoats – not only do they look quite wrong but they must feel quite wrong! Track suits, although perhaps not particularly elegant, are ideal for the job. Not only do they save your own clothes but if you get splashed what does it matter? Don't forget that chlorine, even very diluted in water, can bleach your clothes very easily. I am told that if you do a lot of swimming teaching you may be able to claim an allowance on your income tax for special clothing – an expense incurred wholly, exclusively and necessarily in the performance of your duties!

A class should never exceed 20. Ideally 10 or 12 children make a better class but with water space at a premium one cannot always achieve the ideal. With beginners I think that it is better to take half the number for half the allotted time than to take the whole group for the whole time. Opinions have varied on whether it is better to take a child to the baths once a week for ten or twelve weeks or once a day for a fortnight. I think that the majority now favour the latter and believe in 'a little and often'. This is a problem which affects those using public baths far more than the more fortunate ones with their own bath.

I have never seen it suggested that the children in a school should be divided into swimming 'sets' and yet this is a very logical step to take as it is probably far easier to take a group of fairly good swimmers and a group of the beginners than it is to take two groups of mixed ability. On the other hand the better swimmers are often very willing to help the others, and the poorer ones gain experience from watching and trying to follow the example of the better ones. If you do sort them out by ability then do bear in mind the age and the size of the children. A large older boy who cannot swim gains little from finding himself in the same group as a small young girl who also cannot swim – indeed it may make him feel very self-conscious and the fear of not doing the right thing might so easily deter him from learning altogether. However one finds that one has to take a mixed group, mixed in ability and by sex, from a particular class. With younger children there is no self-consciousness between the sexes but if told to find a partner they generally find one of the same sex. It makes a natural and simple division of a mixed class to say 'I want the boys to watch how the girls do this. Now it's the boys' turn.' Although one wants the children to be at home in the water it is not always a good thing if a child always picks his or her 'best friend' for a partner. An aquatic Paul Jones might be the answer!

Although there are advocates of individual teaching rather than group teaching I think that there must be some group teaching and some working in pairs with the teacher helping individuals when the occasion arises. When I say group teaching I do not mean class teaching as such, with everyone doing the same thing at the same time. We do tend sometimes to over-teach. A child will not learn unless it wants to do so and enjoys doing so, and it is up to us to encourage the child to want to know how to do something. Children like working in groups – they take a pride in their own particular group and they like to compete with and against other groups. They do their best not to 'let the side down'.

In any group of children which we take swimming for the first time there are always some who have been before with their parents or friends and there are always a few who have never been in a swimming bath before. So for the first one or two visits our aim will be to get the children into the water, to get them used to it and to get them to be friends with it. This is known as gaining water confidence and as soon as a child has this then he is almost swimming. Some children have a natural aptitude and no fear (but keep an eye on these because they are inclined to over-estimate their ability!) and others are very hesitant. Don't try to force these hesitant ones into the water – let them sit on the side watching if they wish and if you fail to coax them into the water you will often find that one of their friends will succeed where you have failed.

Having generalized on the teaching of swimming, in the next chapters I will try to go into more detail. As I have said a teacher is an individual, what suits one does not always suit another and there is no right way of teaching swimming although ideas do change from time to time. Make the best and fullest use of the facilities you may have.

Chapter 4: The First Time In

(a) Baths Procedure

1. *Undress quietly and quickly*. Many children regard a visit to the baths as an 'outing' for they associate swimming with a day at the seaside or an afternoon outing with their parents. They may feel that they are free to do what they like and to be as noisy as they like. But there must be a certain discipline for the common good. Perhaps one should not use the word 'quickly' here because most children seem able to undress in 90 seconds flat (although they take a lot longer to get dressed!). It might be better to say 'Undress quietly and neatly' because it is so much easier to step out of one's clothes and drop them on the ground. When the time to dress again arrives, particularly with the younger children, a lot of precious time is wasted sorting out damp pants and vests and socks – it is amazing how much underwear is bought from a certain store and how alike grey socks can be! If the clothes are put down reasonably tidily then a lot of argument and time is saved.

2. *Use the toilets*. Probably an unnecessary piece of advice but all part of the drill. Do blow your nose before leaving the dressing room – you do not carry your handkerchief into the water with you!

3. *Use the shower or footbath*. A showerbath is not always available at the swimming bath but if there is one do use it. There should be a footbath in every pool and entry to the pool should be through the footbath which should be kept disinfected and the water changed at frequent intervals. The chlorination and filtration plant do a most efficient job but attention to personal hygiene by all those who use the bath does help to maintain the efficiency of the plant.

4. *Come clean*. There are still those who think that going to the swimming baths excuses them from having a bath! There is no such thing as 'good, honest dirt' which we sometimes hear spoken about. Very often this good honest dirt contains far more germs than any other form of dirt. Ensure that hands and knees are clean before setting out for the bath and no dirty child should be allowed into the water.

5. *F.F.I.* An F.F.I. was the official army term for a medical inspection to make sure the person was free from infection. At the start of each lesson there should be a brief but searching F.F.I. Most children are fairly conscientious and will tell you if they know there is something wrong with them. But you must be on the look out for open sores, athlete's foot and verrucas but it is not always easy to spot these things. If there is any doubt then medical advice should be sought and swimming forbidden until the child is cleared by the doctor. It does sometimes seem a bit hard to stop a child going swimming when he is perfectly fit apart from a foot infection but it is the duty of everyone to keep the bath free from any form of contamination.

6. *No entry*. No child may enter the water without the consent of the teacher in charge. Fairly obvious no doubt, but the teacher is responsible for the safety of those in his charge and it would be all too easy for an accident to happen in a brief moment of non-supervision. There must be no running on any part of the bath surround – those who do this are a menace to themselves and to others.

7. *Stop!* I suggest that you adopt the practice of when the whistle is blown once it means 'Stop and Listen'. In a teaching bath this presents no problems but in a large bath with a deep end it should not be taken too literally. Someone may be attempting his first length and reached the middle of the deep end – the sudden command to stop might be fatal! It perhaps could mean that the child should stop what it is doing and get to the nearest side and listen. It is not always easy for girls with bathing caps on to hear the whistle and so it must be used with discrimination. Again there must be immediate obedience for one never knows when an emergency might arise and urgent action be needed.

8. *Conclusion.* It may seem that I have belaboured these points and you are possibly asking yourself if there will be any time left for the lesson itself! The whole procedure should not take more than a minute or two and with experience it becomes automatic not only to yourself but to the children.

(b) Water Confidence

The most important stage in the teaching of swimming is to give the child confidence when he is in the water. What do we mean by water confidence? I think that the answer can be given in three parts.

1. *Confidence in the water.* The child will understand that things will

float in water, some things better than others. They can play with bits of different materials, e.g. balsa wood, oak, cork, polystyrene, and will find that there is quite a variation in the way in which these things float. There is little point in telling young children that the specific gravity of different things varies considerably. One has to get them to believe that the human body will float although most of it will be below the surface of the water. One has also to get them to understand that different people float more easily than others, that girls generally float more easily than boys and that the flatter the body is on the water the easier it is to float.

2. *Confidence in the teacher.* Most children have every confidence in their teacher and when taking the newcomers to the baths one must justify this confidence. Keep the children happy and interested with lots of activity however simple the activity may be. If they are relaxed and are enjoying what they are doing they do not build up tensions within themselves. If you are undergoing any medical treatment and are told to relax you know how difficult this can be and for a child to relax consciously is almost an impossibility It is little use telling them to be relaxed but when they are active and warm and enjoying themselves they will relax automatically.

3. *Confidence in themselves.* To have confidence in themselves I think is the most important. Some children are very self-confident and with them the greatest danger is that they will perhaps become over-confident and take risks. But other children need a lot of encouragement to begin with and so be very generous with your praise. For a timid child to put his face under water for the first time may take a tremendous amount of courage and if he is praised for doing it he will feel that he has achieved something wonderful. So make the early exercises simple but make them progressive so that the child feels he is making progress all the time for a sense of achievement is the greatest incentive for a beginner.

(c) Artificial Aids

This may not be quite the right place to talk about the use of artificial aids but if I deal with them now any future reference will perhaps be a little clearer.

There are still two quite distinct schools of thought about the value of using artificial aids in the teaching of swimming, those in favour and those against. I believe that they can be most useful to very many children and, indeed, to older people. There has always been a very strong feeling amongst certain teachers of swimming that it is not 'cricket' to use swimming aids. What is the purpose of using these aids? I think that the main value is that they give the learner an early opportunity of getting his feet off the bottom with his head above water and the satisfaction of being able to move easily through the water. Not all children need to use them, many can discard them after a very short time and there are some who will want to use them for quite a time. They are ideal for practising certain movements, e.g. the leg kick when perhaps you want the children to concentrate on these movements and not to have to worry about what their arms are doing. Many of these aids are adjustable and give less and less support until the time comes when they are discarded altogether. Some aids are simple in construction but effective in action; others are more complicated and so lose some of their efficiency. There are still some advocates of lots of land drill (and the operative word is really drill – everything done by numbers!) before taking the children to the baths. I think that with the use of artificial aids all these practices can be done in the water, in the element in which they have to be used. Is getting a partner to help you using an artificial aid? The purists say that it is but I think that a partner can be a great help on many occasions.

Those who do not advocate the use of these aids say that they rob a child of any confidence he may have and the beginner will rely on them to keep him afloat – they should be supported by the water and not by anything else. This may be true and they are entitled to their opinion. Many children will not need them but they can be a help even to the best swimmer. What parent taking a young child to the baths for the first time does not hold the hands of the child to start with? I have had many children who, in spite of all my efforts and encouragement, have stayed in a corner of the bath shivering but unwilling to give in and get dressed! With the use of various aids, of their own choice, they have moved across the bath with their shoulders down and their feet on the bottom to start with and very soon they have swum a width still using their aid. In a very short time they have discarded the aid and swum a width and then a length and become the keenest in the class. But as I have said earlier this is a matter of individual choice and it is up to the teacher to decide what he thinks is best.

If you are not against using artificial aids then perhaps the following brief descriptions of some of the different types of aid will help you. If you do use them, have a good supply available with you during every lesson – you are not bound to use them. Many Baths Managers allow the local education authorities to keep a supply of floats etc. in boxes or wire mesh baskets at the baths for the use of all their schools using the baths – this does cut down the expense and saves a lot of carrying to and from the baths.

1. *Rope and halter.* I am personally very much against the use of a rope and halter. Very many times have I seen a small child dragged through the water on the end of one of these things – the child too frightened to do anything except pray that they will soon reach the other end of the bath! I remember seeing a taut wire fixed across the width of the bath with a large pulley wheel resting on it. Through the wheel a rope was passed with the unlucky child suspended on one end with a webbing strap somewhere round his middle and the teacher attached to the other. The idea was that the child was held up in the water while he practised his stroke and as he grew more proficient the rope was lowered and gave him less support. Probably in the last fifty years hundreds of people have been taught to swim this way but it is not for me!

2. *Buoyancy aids.* These come in various shapes and sizes and their main advantage is that they are worn on the person leaving the arms and legs free. Many years ago, when manufacturers had not appreciated the big market there would be, a friend of mine collected a quantity of flat tins, e.g. petrol or large syrup tins, painted them in bright colours, sealed them to make them airtight and fastened them on to a wide belt. The belt was fastened round the child's waist. These were most effective buoyancy aids. Now there are many types of more sophisticated buoyancy aids.

I must add a word of warning here. However good and however effective these aids are for the teaching of swimming in a swimming bath they must never be used in open waters or the sea unless the user is very closely supervised. The inflatable type are particularly dangerous because they can become deflated and then all support is gone. False confidence changes to panic and life may be lost.

There are a variety of aids on the market now but it is up to the individual to decide what type to use, although one should not be restricted to one type alone. Perhaps the following brief descriptions may encourage you to try out some of them.

(a) *Rubber rings*. These have been used for very many years and may be seen decking the stalls at seaside resorts by the hundreds in every variety of colour and shape. Unfortunately many of these are of poor quality and their life is limited and so it is false economy to buy cheap ones. Initially they are quite useful because they give the user freedom to move in the water and be well supported but they do restrict arm and leg movement when swimming strokes are attempted. Inflated car tubes can give the same help but are more unwieldy.

(b) *Arm bands*. The first arm bands were designed by Mr Reg. Brickett, a founder member and the first Hon. Secretary of the Swimming Teachers Association. He has used them most successfully with learners of all ages. They are inflatable bands worn on the upper arms. The amount of air in the bands can be regulated to give more or less buoyancy as required. They are extremely useful as they can support the user and yet give freedom of movement. They are now produced by many firms and vary in design. Some are of the single band type and others have a double band both parts being inflatable separately. Recently a new type has been produced and these have a flat side which is worn between the arm and the body.

(c) *Floats*. Again there are a great variety of these. Years ago they were made of cork but in recent years polystyrene has been used. These are very light and give ample support. Their drawback is that they are so attractive to look at that children are tempted to nibble at them and pieces get broken off and these pieces can block filtration plants! One firm uses a special lightweight covering for these polystyrene floats which gives them added strength to withstand the wear and tear of daily use. Some very good floats we have used are made from a composition called plastazote. These floats are strong, well finished and give good support.

Floats can be used in a variety of different ways and probably the children will find many ways which you haven't even thought of! Their main use is in supporting the arms and are held in the hands which are stretched out in front. This is of great help in practising the leg kicks. One may be held under each arm with the user lying on the back and this helps to keep the head out of the water which, in the initial stages, is most important from the beginner's point of view. When practising the arm movements of the back crawl a float may be held between the knees. Most of these floats are about 12 inches long by 8 inches wide and the average cost is about 10/- each. Many education authorities purchase the floats in bulk quantities which reduces the price considerably.

(d) *Stubton Float Suit.* The Stubton Float Suit is a swimming costume which is worn over ordinary swimwear. It has pockets sewn on to it and these pockets are capable of holding small polystyrene floats up to 12 in number. The wearer is given as much flotation as is required to support him in a floating position and so he is able to concentrate on learning to swim. The great advantage of this float suit is that the amount of buoyancy given can be so easily adjusted by adding or removing the floats. The position of the buoyancy can also be regulated. With most people the full number of floats is not required but much depends on the wearer. A timid beginner can wear the suit with full floats and can be encouraged to move round in a sitting position until he has achieved some free leg kicking and arm splashing. The learner is then encouraged to make more positive movements with the arms and legs and to use his mouth for breathing – at this stage there need be no attempt at co-ordination. As the wearer gains strength in movement then one or two floats may be removed and this can be continued until finally the wearer can 'swim' with no support at all. The floats can then be re-inserted and practice can be given in improving the arm and leg movements and in their co-ordination. By repeating the process of removing the floats by degrees the wearer will find that he is able to swim quite well and the need of the float suit is gone. The Stubton Float Suit is produced in all sizes from 22" to 40" chest.

(e) *Flippers.* Those of you who have used flippers in the water know how much more leg power they can give you and also a sense of freedom of movement. There is still a feeling that it is 'not done' to use flippers to help a child to learn to swim but if they will give him enough confidence to propel himself through the water why not let him use them? Anything which is worn rather than held is of great advantage for the arms and legs are then free to be put to their proper purpose.

(*f*) *Swim belts etc.* Basically a swim belt is a belt to which is attached a float or buoyancy aid of some description. Some floats have two holes in them through which a belt can be passed. Some belts have a polystyrene float fixed to them and others have blocks, perhaps two in front and two behind, which are removable individually when confidence is gained. Then there are small jackets with built-in buoyancy worn over the shoulders and tied at the waist. These all have some value as they are worn and do not impede movement of arms and legs.

(*g*) *Music.* It seems rather strange to include music as an artificial aid in the teaching of swimming. Teachers are well aware of the value of the 'music and movement' approach for young children to physical education – this approach has been made so popular by the B.B.C. series which has been broadcast for many years. Why not use a similar approach in the swimming bath? It might not be very practical in a public baths but there is no reason why it could not be attempted in a school pool. If one chooses a lively popular tune then the children feel that it is a natural play situation and forget the fact that they are in the water. If they are all provided with armbands they can move around freely to the music. A variety of exercises leading on to the first stages of leg and arm swimming movements can be worked out to fit in with the particular pieces of music chosen. As a conclusion to the lesson the children could be asked to produce their own activity to fit in with the music and I am sure that one would find that some excellent movements were produced.

(*h*) *Bamboo poles.* In the past I have found that a bamboo pole of $1''$ or $1\frac{1}{2}''$ diameter is a most useful piece of equipment. It should be about 10 or 12 feet long. Poles of this sort are used by carpet manufacturers to roll carpets round before sending them to the shops and I am sure that you can find some shopkeeper with a kindly disposition who will give you one or two. I have never seen any but there must be poles of this sort made from plastic on the market – these would be even more suitable as they would be light, strong and smooth.

They can be used for a variety of pushing and pulling games, for jumping over from the side or for ducking under in the water. I have found them useful for practising leg kicks with perhaps three children each side. The pole can be supported at each end or the children can try to move the pole against the opposition from the other side using only the legs.

(i) *Conclusion.* The use of aids of any sort is again a matter for the individual teacher who knows the limitations of the facilities and the children he is teaching. I do not think that there is anything wrong in using artificial aids as long as they achieve the purpose for which we are using them and that is, in the main, to help the children to be at home and happy in the water right from the beginning. When the time comes they can be weaned from their use quite easily – some children will have little need of them, others may need them for quite a time. As they become good swimmers they will be using artificial aids again as so many of our top swimmers do, at least so the advertisements tell us! They use floats for practising leg kicks, arm fins for giving greater strength and endurance by building up the swimming muscles and inflatable anklets for isolating the legs when practising arm movements.

May I repeat my warning that, however good these aids may be, they should not be used in open waters or in the sea unless the wearer is very closely supervised. They are a potential danger because of tides and currents over which we have no control.

Chapter 5: Attainment Tests

What a formidable title to a chapter in a book on the teaching of swimming to the young! To many of us these words recall the tests of the bad old days devised as a means of separating the sheep from the goats! I assure you that I mean nothing of the kind!

The first time a child opens its eyes under water, lets go of the side or walks across the shallow end of the bath – these are all attainments and I believe they should be recognized. You can reward a child as you will, by a star, a housepoint or a piece of coloured ribbon, and these rewards, though very small to us mean such a lot to a child. Attainments or skills can be rewarded individually or in groups. Each child can have its own record on which the skill achieved is ticked off or a card on which there are ten things to do and when the ten are done a special award is made.

When the child can struggle across the width of the bath without its feet touching the bottom then it has taken the first important step to becoming a swimmer – a school certificate should be awarded although one should try to avoid calling the child a swimmer at this stage. To be able to swim 25 yards is recognized by most authorities as a qualification for a swimmer. Many local education authorities and schools' swimming associations issue certificates for this and greater distances. The A.S.A. and E.S.S.A., as part of their Joint Swimming Awards Scheme, issue attractive certificates for bulk buying by local authorities (for details apply to the Organizer for A.S.A. – see Appendix A).

I have seen a variety of swimming progress boards in schools – some most attractive. There must be some artistic members of your staff who will design such a board for your school. We have used such a board, divided into columns, decorated with underwater scenes. In the first column are the minnows, the children who can swim a width, and as they progress to a length, 50 yards, 100 yards and so on they become bigger and bigger fish. Very simple, but it does seem to encourage the children.

The following simple tests of skills may be used to encourage the beginner and as a basis for 'rewards'. They may be combined to form progress or attainment cards. They are not in a particular order but they all lead to preparing the child to be ready to swim.

1. Sit on bath side, kicking and splashing with feet.
2. Sit on top step then gradually move down into water.
3. Sit on bath side, get into water holding hand of partner in water.
4. Sit on bath side, turn round and lower oneself into water.
5. Walk down steps and into water.
6. Walk across shallow end of bath holding rail.
7. Walk across shallow end holding partner's hand.
8. Walk across shallow end without holding anything.
9. Sit on bathside, jump in.
10. Crouch on bath side, jump in.
11. Stand on bath side, jump in.
12. Stand in water, bend knees until shoulders are under and chin on water.
13. Stand in water, bend and splash face.
14. Hold rail bobbing up and down until shoulders submerged.
15. Without holding rail bobbing up and down.
16. Hold rail bobbing up and down until head is under water.
17. Face in water, blow bubbles.
18. Submerge head, open eyes under water, count partner's fingers.
19. Without holding bobbing up and down with head submerged.
20. Kneel on bottom or, if too deep, crouch, allowing arms to float up.
21. Sit on bottom of bath.
22. Blow a table tennis ball on surface of water for 6 feet.
23. Pick up objects from bottom of bath.
24. Walk across bath bending from hips, shoulders submerged, using arms to pull through the water.
25. Shoulders under water, arms forward and pull back.
26. Shoulders under, lean forward, jump with two feet as you pull with arms. Recover and stand.
27. Lean right forward, good pull to standing position.
28. Lean forward, pull and let legs follow into glide.
29. Lean forward, glide and recover.

ATTAINMENT TESTS

30. Lean forward and, with good push off the bottom, glide and recover.
31. Hold partner's waist and be towed across bath.
32. Hold partner's waist and be towed kicking with legs.
33. Lean forward into prone floating position.
34. Lean forward, mushroom float position, and recover.
35. Lean forward, glide and kick with legs.
36. Use float glide and kick with legs.
37. Lean back in water and recover.
38. Lean back into back float position and scull with hands.
39. Hold rail, feet up, push back into float position and scull.
40. Prone glide pushing off with feet from wall of bath.
41. Prone position, push off from side to reach bottom of bath.
42. Prone, glide with float, simple crawl leg kick.
43. Prone, glide with float, breast stroke kick.
44. Floats under arms, push off, back crawl leg kick.
45. Floats under arms, push off, life-saving leg kick.
46. Prone, glide with float, double leg kick as for Dolphin.
47. From crouch, using arms only, breast stroke.
48. Walk across bath using arms for crawl stroke, head low.
49. As 48 letting legs trail.
50. As 47 and 48 using float between legs, arm practices.
51. Sit on bath side, head-first entry pushing off from rail.
52. Kneel on one knee, head-first entry.
53. Crouch on bath side, head-first entry.
54. Swim three strokes and surface dive.
55. Handstand on bottom of bath.
56. Forward somersault from standing position.
57. Dive over a pole held at water level.
58. Dive through a hoop held below water.
59. From glide forward roll through water.
60. Push off from side on back, glide, backward roll.
62. Dive through partner's legs.
63. Swim, glide and surface dive to pick up coin from bath bottom.
64. Swim a width under water.
65. Swim for one or two minutes with no feet on bottom and without touching sides.
66. Swim or float on back for one minute.

67. Swim a width crawl stroke on one breath.
68. Swim a width breast stroke with only three strokes.

Many other tests can be devised on the lines of the above. I have not included the more recognized tests e.g. one width crawl legs only, one width breast, one length free style, one length back stroke. Tests can be graded in difficulty. Progress cards should have only a limited number of tests on each, perhaps six, and there should be variety in each group. These tests need not involve you in much clerical work. They can be duplicated on to sheets, cut into sections and pasted on to cards. What little extra work for you will be caused will be well recompensed by the interest and the progress of the children.

Chapter 6: Having Fun!

Games and Activities
During every swimming lesson there should be a few minutes for some form of relaxation when one might introduce one or two short games or activities. Not only are these good for relaxation but they all help with water confidence. Most games used in the P.E. lesson may be adapted for use in the swimming bath. It might not always be practical if using a public bath and perhaps sharing the water space with another school or even with the general public but if you are fortunate to have your own pool then the following reminders might be of some value to you.

(a) *Touch or Tag.* The one who is 'He' or 'It' has to touch one of the others. The one who is touched becomes 'He'. You may not be caught if e.g. your feet are off the bottom of the bath or you are completely under the water.

A variation is when one is caught he joins hands with his catcher, the third one to be caught also joins hands but when there are four they split into two twos and so on until all are caught.

(b) *Follow the leader.* The leader can do what he likes, walk, swim, float etc. and everyone has to follow what he does.

(c) *Here, there and where.* When the teacher calls 'Here' the children swim towards him, when it is 'There' they swim in the direction to which he points and when it is 'Where' they jump up and down in the water, or float, or any variation you like.

(d) *Ring-a-roses.* This needs no explanation but be careful that a nervous child does not get pulled over, perhaps backwards.

(e) *Cranes and crows.* Children in two lines standing in centre of bath, one line being the crows and the other the cranes. Whichever line is called chase the others who try to get to the edge of the pool without being touched.

(*f*) *Horse and jockey.* A double ring of children. On the word 'go' the children in the inner ring turn round, crawl or dive through their partner's legs, run or swim round the outside of the circle and jump on to their partner's back. The first one up is the winner.

(*g*) *Knights on horseback.* One child is the horse and his partner gets on his back. The aim is to pull off the other knights. Only volunteers should play this!

(*h*) *Tunnel race.* The teams line up with feet astride and well-spaced. On 'go' the first one turns round, crawls or swims through the second one's legs and so on down the line. When he gets to the end he stands behind the last one with legs apart. In the meantime as soon as the first one has gone through the second one's legs the second one turns round and follows the first one. The team first back to the original order wins. Four or five in a team are enough.

(*i*) *Tug of war.* This can be done in a variety of ways. A rope could be used but I would suggest a long bamboo pole with two each side holding on to the pole and swimming with legs only to push the other side backwards.

(*j*) *Net ball.* No net but for want of a better name! An inner tube at each end of the bath. The ball has to drop into the ring for a goal to be scored. I suggest that the ball should only be thrown when child is swimming. For this make your own rules!

(*k*) *Chinese Wall.* I am not sure if this is the right name but it will do. The children line up in water at side of bath with one in the centre. The children try to cross from one side to the other. If caught they stay in middle to try to catch the others. Last one to be caught the winner!

(*l*) *Relay races.* Any number of varieties!
  (i) Free style relays.
  (ii) Medley relays e.g. breast stroke, back stroke and crawl or alternate ones doing back stroke.
  (iii) Walking race, either forward or backward.
  (iv) Ball relay, passing ball back and forth to leader.
  (v) Leap frog relay – if water is not too deep. It makes a good splash on landing.

HAVING FUN!

- (vi) Blowing a table tennis ball relay.
- (vii) Towing relay. Each team has an inner tube attached to a rope. The rope and tube are thrown by leader, who holds on to one end of rope, to second member of team who has to climb into the tube and be pulled back to leader who then throws it back to No. 3 and so on.
- (viii) Pushing relay with partners. One partner sits in an inner tube and is pushed by partner to line either to win or a second pair can take over back to starting line.
- (ix) Baton relay. Instead of a baton the children use a float. The first child swims using the float which is then passed on to second child who swims back to third member of team and so on until the whole team have had a turn.
- (x) Boat race. Three variations.

    The simplest variation is where children are in line with hands on each other's shoulders. The race is from one end or side of bath to the other. If the team break their hold then they have to go back to beginning and start again. This is a walking race.

    The teams line up holding each other round the waist. The team leader, who is the cox, faces his team and holds the hands of the No. 1. It is a good idea to have them with bent knees and shoulders at water level. On the start the teams jump forward together in short jumps taking their time from the cox.

    The teams lie on their backs with their feet tucked under the armpits of the ones in front. The arms are used for propulsion and the last swimmer uses legs as well. If they break from each other they start again.
- (xi) Tunnel ball relay. This can be fun but the ball cannot be rolled between legs but must be passed underneath. As a variation the ball can be passed overhead or over and under.

(*m*) *Bull in the ring.* Groups of four or five with one in centre. One stands in centre of ring formed by others joining hands. On the signal the bull tries to get out of the ring. Perhaps this is more suitable for boys than girls – or is it?

(*n*) *One against three.* Groups of four with three joining hands to form a circle and the remaining player runs round outside of circle trying to touch one of the three who has been named. The circle may move about anywhere. Each of the players takes it in turn to be outside.

Some swimming skills
(a) Somersaults. Both forward and backward.
(b) Submarine. Floating on back with arm or leg raised as periscope.
(c) Starfish. Floating face downward with arms and legs outstretched.
(d) Sculling. Lying on back. Using hands only for propulsion.
(e) Tandem swimming. Swimming in pairs either on back or face downward. One uses legs and the other arms for propulsion.
(f) Mushroom floating. This is going to be the only swimming book in which this is not described!
(g) Treading water. Remaining in an upright position in same spot. Not easy in shallow water but it can be done with knees bent.
(h) Undressing in water. Children find it fun to bring old pyjamas, shirts or blouses and shorts and perhaps socks and then trying to undress in the water without touching bottom. They can practise the inflation of their discarded clothes to use as floats. This is an excellent preliminary practice for survival swimming and awards.
(i) Swimming to music. As suggested earlier this can be fun. With a portable tape recorder or an extension speaker and some bright music let the swimmers make their own movements to the music. The non-swimmers can join in standing in circles or pairs bending and turning in the water to the music. This is a good introduction to synchronized swimming.
(j) Underwater swimming. Swimming through hoops held in position on bath bottom with attached brick. Recovering coins or bricks from bath bottom.

Chapter 7: Artistic Executions

You might well ask why have I chosen such an odd title to a chapter in a book on swimming! I had to find some title and this is perhaps a little intriguing and has got you wondering. Artistic executions is the definition given in one dictionary for the word techniques – hence the use of this title.

I do want to say a few words about teaching techniques and although you may not agree with what I say I hope that it might help you to crystallize your own ideas. May I say that I am not trying to impose my ideas on you. Each individual teacher has his own ideas and his own personality and these must dictate which method he will use, for certain techniques suit only a certain type of person. But everyone should be prepared to try out the ideas of others and possibly to adapt their own ideas. The secret of success is, I believe, that whatever method is used it is the keenness and enthusiasm of the teacher which is the main and most important factor.

I said that I was not going to go into details on the teaching of each stroke in this book – there are so many books available which deal in detail with this and they are written by people who are far more expert at teaching swimming than I am. So this chapter, which perhaps should be one of many long chapters on the teaching of strokes, will be fairly brief and deal only with generalities.

If one picks up almost any book on the teaching of swimming published prior to the Second World War one finds that almost as much stress is placed on the teaching of land drill as on teaching in the water. Personally I think that land drills are almost a complete waste of time in the teaching of beginners. The only time that one can really justify their use is when one wishes to correct perhaps an arm movement of a swimmer which is not quite right in the water.

What of the techniques used today to teach children to swim? There are several and I should like to mention them briefly as there is something to be said for all of them.

(a) Methods

1. *The single stroke method.* This is perhaps still the most used method as it is perhaps the easiest when dealing with a large class. It has one great drawback which is that there is the danger of a teacher imposing a particular stroke on a child which is not the most suitable stroke for that particular child. There is always the controversy about which is the best stroke to teach first. Some believe that the crawl stroke, which is a form of extension of the dog paddle, is the more natural stroke to teach first. Others believe that the breast stroke is easier for children to learn and there are some who think that it is easier to swim on the back.

2. *The many-stroke method.* This method does cater for the individual in the class. A variety of strokes are introduced at an early stage so that the child can work on any one of his choice or on all strokes at the same time. The difficulty here is in the control of the class and the organization of the work of the class.

3. *Teaching with artificial aids.* The main purpose of this method is to get the child moving in the water, practising arm and leg movements, for he will have overcome his lack of confidence in his ability to keep his head above the water. It is, of course, far better to have something to wear rather than to hold. Quite recently I saw a demonstration of swimming teaching where there were dozens of five- and six-year-olds, complete with rubber rings, being taught to swim in a large bath and many of them were in the diving pool with over twelve feet of water. Before the end of the lesson several of the latter had discarded their rings and were swimming about quite happily over eight feet away from the side.

4. *Teaching by the shallow water method.* This is a method which was devised and used with great success by Mrs Winifred Gibson. Children are taught in water which is shallow enough for them to put their hands on the bottom when in the horizontal position. It is probably the method by which the quickest results are obtained. The great difficulty about this method is in getting the right facilities for it for you must have a pool where at least some of the water is 18 to 24 inches deep. If a pool is built in this way then it has great limitations when all the users can swim. It is possible to lower the water in a teaching swimming bath to use this method.

5. *Drownproofing.* This is perhaps not a method of teaching swimming as we understand the meaning of the word but it is a skill of vital

importance for it teaches the subject to remain on the surface of the water comfortably and for an indefinite length of time. It is a means of personal safety and its success depends on the subject discovering the natural buoyancy of the body and proper breathing. If we have our priorities right then perhaps we should teach drownproofing before any strokes. The survival method using flotation techniques has been used in the United States for years and the aim has been from the start to teach survival rather than swimming as the first priority.

6. *Individual instruction*. All the foregoing methods are suitable for individual teaching. I have recently read an article on how they teach children in the Far East to swim by throwing them into the water on the end of a rope! So many of them live on boats that they must learn to swim at a very early age to survive and although this method is a drastic one it must be effective although I am not advocating it. I cannot remember how I learnt to swim but of one thing I am certain and that is I was never taught and I did most of my swimming in places which would horrify me if I found my own children using them!

Schools with their own pools have a great advantage because there are often odd moments during the day when individual children can be given some instruction. Many of them will benefit from just a few minutes on their own with their teacher, just as in any other subject, and I am referring here, of course, to the children who are nervous perhaps or who have been away during early stages and not to the good swimmers. Again, with individual teaching just as with class teaching, the teacher must use whichever method he thinks most suitable for himself and for the particular child.

(b) The Development of Swimming Strokes

At the stage when one is going to develop the swimming strokes of the beginner it must be assumed that the child is fairly confident in the water and has a knowledge of the simple skills such as being able to glide, immerse the head and open the eyes under water. Some children will have progressed far more than others and the general suggestions here will not apply to all children to the same degree. It is suggested that before the introduction of any new stroke a visual example of the stroke should be given either by a good swimmer or a film. This will give the child some idea of what he is supposed to be trying to do.

Before introducing a new stroke it is suggested that the class should be divided into perhaps three groups so that the work might progress at different rates. The three groups would be

1. The naturals – those who are already quite good.
2. The average ones who with guidance and practice will become good.
3. The very slow starters who need lots of help and encouragement and who may never become good swimmers.

Having given your visual example of the stroke which is being introduced the following points are to be aimed at in your lessons.

1. *Basic Stroke.* There are variations on the basic stroke so pick out the fundamentals. Teach the common factors of the stroke and then each child will adapt them to suit him or herself.

2. *Results.* By getting the basic details first you will begin to get immediate results which, although they may not be perfect in style, will give the child encouragement to improve by practising the various parts of the stroke.

3. *Progressive Practices.* The five fundamentals in each stroke have to be practised as separate skills and then as a whole. The amount of practice needed will vary with each individual and in some cases may not be necessary.

In each stroke the five fundamentals are

1. Body position
2. Leg action
3. Arm action
4. Breathing
5. Timing.

Water Mechanics. Before going into any detail about applying the above fundamentals to each stroke one should consider why they are important to the swimmer. In the mechanics of swimming there are two main factors:

1. Resistance
2. Propulsion

1. *Resistance*

(a) Frontal body area resistance. The 'blunt end' of a ship is always at the back because if it was not there would be far more resistance to the water because of its larger area. The same applies to the human body and one must aim to cut down this resistance. The head must be kept well down and the body as flat as possible in the water.

Because of the lack of correct practice beginners tend to keep the head high as they do not appreciate what a big muscular effort is required to do this and what resistance is caused.
(b) Individual resistance. There are two factors which can only be overcome by the individual:
   (i) Hair resistance. Perhaps this is not great but it has some effect and it is therefore better to wear a cap.
   (ii) Costume resistance. Some of you may have experienced the sense of freedom of having swum without wearing a costume and in fact a costume does cause quite a lot of resistance. The material makes quite a lot of difference – it should be light and not shiny but slightly matt. Girls' costumes should be high at the neck for if they are low they act as an effective drogue.
(c) Low pressure eddies. These are factors which perhaps are beyond the individual to control but the wrong movements of the arms and body can cause some of them.
(d) Effect of bow wave. Any object moving through water causes a bow wave and although one cannot cut it out altogether the best way of minimizing its effect is to get as much of the body under the water as possible.

2. *Propulsion*

Propulsion is the act of driving forward and to send a person forward in the water there must be a backward movement. In other words to every action there must be a reaction. One may compare one's movement through the water with that of a canoe where, as the paddle is pulled backwards, the canoe shoots forward. The result of the effect of a paddle is always at right angles and as the arms pull downwards and backwards the body moves forward. In swimming we use a variety of paddle actions – in the arm movements of the front and back crawl and in the breaststroke and butterfly and also in the leg action of the breaststroke.

In the earlier days of the aeroplane the propeller action caused the plane to move forward just as the rotor-blades of a helicopter causes it to move upwards. So in swimming we use this propeller effect with the hands and arms in sculling and in the leg strokes of the back and front crawl in the butterfly dolphin.

3. *The principle of leverage*

In addition to the two forms of mechanics mentioned above we do also apply the principles of leverage. The arm is a lever and we shorten this lever by bending the arm and so get less power. We must therefore stretch the arms to the fullest extent except in recovery strokes. If the upper body is strong then we can use straighter arms. If we cup our hands or open our fingers then we are decreasing the size of our paddles and lessening the pull through the water.

(c) The Strokes

Because there is so much competitive swimming at all levels taking place these days we are inclined to think that there are only four strokes in swimming, the breast, butterfly, front and back crawl. There are however two strokes which do not appear in the competitive field but I think that it is very important that they should be learnt and practised because they are of great value in survival swimming and life-saving. These are the life-saving back stroke, with or without the use of arms and with a leg kick which is almost the reverse of the breast stroke kick, and the side stroke which is no longer fashionable and which is supposed to encourage unequal development of the body. The side stroke is probably less strenuous than any other stroke and can be kept up for long distances. The position of the swimmer's head allows more regular breathing in the rougher waters. Unfortunately achievement in swimming is recognized only by ability in the four main strokes except in life-saving and survival swimming and so, once again, we have perhaps got our priorities wrong. I hope that schools will be able to introduce these two strokes at some time in their swimming lessons.

The Breast Stroke
1. Try out the swimmers. Divide them into three groups.
2. The first concern is for the arm stroke.
3. It is an unnatural stroke for the legs (we aren't frogs!). But the leg stroke will follow the arm stroke almost automatically.
4. Prastise the leg stroke using a float.
5. Practise the life-saving leg stroke on the back.
6. Use land drill only if it is impossible to get the correct actions any other way.

Body position. The body should be as flat as possible although head is slightly raised and so the legs will be a little lower. The eyes look forward either just above or below the water surface.

ARTISTIC EXECUTIONS

Leg action. The power from the leg kick is in the backward drive and not in the squeeze of the legs coming together. The legs are held straight and close together and the feet are extended so that the soles are uppermost but the swimmer should be relaxed. The feet are drawn towards the seat until the heels are almost touching it. The legs must work together otherwise what is known as the screw kick develops. The toes are bent towards the shins and, as the drive with the legs takes place, the heels push against the water, the toes are extended and the soles of the feet are uppermost. The feet come together again and the legs are now in the original glide position with the main thrust having been achieved. As the body moves forward at its maximum speed with the legs together there is a short rest. A strong ankle rotation helps to drive the water backwards and so increase the speed of the swimmer.

Arm action. There can be a variation in the arm action depending on the use of the stroke – for survival, pleasure or speed swimming. Any of these forms is acceptable. The arms should be kept just under the surface of the water and the action should be continuous, fairly shallow and short. From the glide position the arms, which are kept straight, are pulled downwards and outwards until they are roughly at right angles to each other. This action raises the head above the water and this is when breathing takes place. The hands are pulled towards the body, the elbows are bent slightly and brought into the sides of the body and the hands come up under the chin with the palms downwards. The hands are pushed forward, keeping the palms downward and so back to the original glide position. As the arms go forward in an easy motion the exhalation through nose and mouth takes place.

Breathing. Breathing-in takes place with the pulling down of the hands and arms and as the head is automatically raised should present little difficulty. As the arms go forward at the completion of the stroke breathing out takes place. If you suggest to the children that they 'Blow the hands forward' they will get the time about right and it will help to empty the lungs. It does depend somewhat on the nature of the stroke where breathing should take place.

Timing. The timing of the breast stroke almost follows automatically as the arm pull and leg kick alternate. During the arm pull there is no movement of the legs. As the hands are brought up under the chin the legs are drawn up with heels together. As the arms go forward into the glide position the legs drive backwards and straighten out.

Practices. Individual practices should take place in all the above actions and these can take place at the rail, with the use of floats and by walking across the bath with knees bent and shoulders at water level. Having practised all the movements individually and in combination, such as breathing and arms, the whole stroke can be tried. This should be done in a slow and unhurried manner and perhaps the best way is to attempt a width first and then a length in as few strokes as possible. The teacher can, at this stage, help the swimmers by giving the timing and rhythm: pull and breathe in – recover arms and legs – kick and breathe out – glide. If the stroke is done slowly then oral correction can be given where necessary.

The Front Crawl
1. Give a demonstration by a good swimmer. Point out the various actions as they occur.
2. Using the glide to start, leg kick across the bath.
3. Using floats (or rings or flippers) leg kick across bath.
4. Free practice using arms to fit in with leg stroke.

Body position. Head held low in the water with seat down.

Leg action. The leg action is the most important movement in the crawl stroke and should be practised first. If one attempts to do the whole stroke without any practice, the legs tend to trail and the balance of the body is upset. At this stage the head should remain to the front, not turned to the side for breathing. Constant practice must take place with the leg stroke until they drive continuously without any apparent effort. The legs move alternately up and down to a depth of about 12 inches and should be kept under the water with only the heels just breaking the surface. On the downward stroke the leg should bend slightly at the knee with the foot turning slightly inwards. It is the whip-lash action of the feet which gives the propulsion by directing backwards the eddies of water. The legs should move evenly and regularly which gives the steady drive. The depth of the kick will vary with individuals but it should be kept shallow and with little splash. Ankle mobility is most important.

Arm action. The arm action is a windmill action. One arm is pressed downwards and backwards until it reaches the thigh when it is bent and raised until it is clear of the water and then completes the cycle. As the first arm touches the thigh the second arm begins the stroke. The entry

ARTISTIC EXECUTIONS

of the arm should be in the front of the head and should pull down and not sideways. The arms continue in this rhythmic sequence with no pause for rest as in the breast stroke. There can be quite a variation in the entry of the arms depending on the individual.

Breathing. In the early stages it is advisable to breathe once in every complete arm stroke – it is a matter of personal choice on which side one breathes, whichever comes naturally. The head should be turned smoothly without any extra bending of the neck. As the arm on the breathing side passes the face then the head should start to turn. Air should be inhaled through the mouth and exhaled under water through the nose and mouth. The head action should be a smooth movement to avoid rolling and loss of balance and as the breathing is linked with the arm movement it should be a continuous process.

Timing. There are many variations in the timing of the leg kick (perhaps the word kick is not the right one to use as the action is a leg swing from the hips) but it must balance with the arm action. As one arm is starting its downward pull movement the opposite leg is starting its downward kick. Normally there are six beats of the legs to one complete circle of both arms. In the crawl stroke there is a steady and constant propulsion from the unbroken rhythm of the arm and leg movements.

Practices. The leg practices are most important to get the easy swing from the hips and not the kick with the knee bent. These should be started at the rail with a slow tempo which gradually can be increased. Then follows the glide with the leg swing and the use of a float with the hands resting on it for support and with arms straight.

The arm movement is practised from a standing position and then from walking forward keeping the face well down. The same practices are repeated combining the arm action with breathing.

Having found the natural side for breathing this should be practised from the standing and walking positions and during the glide when the arm on the non-breathing side may be supported by a float. Give practice in holding the breath for 10 seconds, then for 5 seconds blowing out as fast as possible. While holding the breath as long as possible try swimming a width and then a length. In short races you will find that experienced swimmers will breathe as seldom as possible.

The Back Crawl

Many people think that the Back Crawl can be taught quite as easily as the Breast Stroke. It is a similar stroke to the Front Crawl except that the body is in the supine position. It is a restful recreational stroke and a most efficient racing stroke. As both strokes are complementary to each other they may be taught simultaneously giving variety in practice.

Body position. One can assume that at this stage the children will have used the back floating position and will have been shown how to regain their feet from this position. The body must be kept flat with the hips up and the head back resting on the water but sufficiently high to keep the face out of the water with the ears just immersed. The eyes should look towards the feet or vertically upward.

Leg action. The legs work up and down alternately and this action helps to give the horizontal position. The depth of the kick must vary with the length of the legs of the swimmer and should be from 18 inches to two feet. As with the Front Crawl it is a swinging action and should be relaxed with the legs more straight than bent. The feet should not break the surface of the water and there should be no splash. The toes should be pointed and turned slightly inwards and ankle mobility exerts a whipping action on the water.

Arm action. The arms work alternately in a continuous movement with one driving as the other is recovering and thus giving smooth propulsion. The point of entry above the head is determined by various factors of the individual e.g. width of shoulders, length of arms, suppleness of shoulders but generally it is slightly wide of the shoulders. The hand enters the water with the little finger first and only when the whole arm is immersed in the water does the pull begin. The arm moves in a semi-circular sideways sweep from the entry until it is lifted out on reaching the thigh. In the recovery from the water the arm can be straight or bent, it can come high or low out of the water and the fingers can be open or closed. About 75 per cent of the propulsion is gained from the action of the arms.

Breathing. There should be little difficulty with breathing as the face of the swimmer is clear of the water and the time of breathing and its nature should be left to each individual. It will become rhythmical and with beginners it is as well to stress the rhythm.

Timing. As with the front crawl the timing should come naturally but the six beat rhythm is the most usual.

Practices. Again the leg practices are most important, Practise gliding on the back with the leg swing, vary it with gliding in prone position and with changing from front to back. Using floats, one under each arm, the leg action should be practised and then dispensing with the floats use the legs with the hands sculling through the water. Following this the hands are placed on the hips. Practice is carried out with the arms above the head but this is most difficult and need not be done before starting the arm action.

It is possible to use the rails or a float between the knees to practise the arm movements but it is better to use legs. Do not assume that the children cannot do the windmill arm movement – let them try it. The continuous movement of the arms should be emphasized. The arms should be stretched back as far as possible. There may be a tendency to go wide and with stiff shoulders one is inclined to roll. If a child cannot do the windmill movement then it can be shown how to do it out of the water – this is one of the few occasions when we should use land drill.

Constant practice using the combined arm and leg movement is necessary and this should be alternated with leg movement practices.

The Butterfly Stroke

This is sometimes called the Butterfly Dolphin or the Dolphin Butterfly Stroke. It is a comparatively new stroke and it was not until 1953 that it was recognized as a stroke in its own right and rules laid down for its performance. After the Second World War breast stroke swimmers found that with an out-of-water arm recovery they could achieve far greater speeds. As laws had not been made to cover the arm recovery in the Breast Stroke this was allowed and so one had the 'orthodox' and 'unorthodox' Breast Stroke swimmers, the latter having a great advantage over the former. The double-arm action was supposed to resemble that of the butterfly but when one sees a butterfly swimmer ploughing down the bath there seems little resemblance to the graceful butterfly. Originally there was a modified breast stroke leg action but this became rather like a double crawl kick and the name dolphin is derived from the large tail action of the dolphin. As a stroke the butterfly is not taught to beginners as a first stroke and is generally not learnt until there is proficiency in the other strokes.

Body position. The body should be kept as near horizontal in the water as possible. By using side breathing or alternate breathing it helps to keep the body in the correct position as it reduces the need to raise and lower the head to breathe. The undulations of the body should be kept to the minimum.

Leg action. The leg action is a simultaneous crawl action and so a knowledge of the crawl stroke is of great help. The legs move upwards together and the knees bend slightly and are opened a little. As the feet come just below the surface of the water the knees are straightened and the legs are brought down vigorously with the toes turned slightly inwards and the feet relaxed. There should be little splash from the feet and the kick should not be very deep. The simultaneous leg action causes the upper part of the body to be raised and this gives the up-and-down movement of the swimmer.

Arm action. The arm action is a double crawl arm action with no pause in the movement. The entry should not be too wide – rather less than shoulder width. If there is not sufficient power then the arm can be bent slightly and the fingers opened or cupped. The arms should be pulled back into line with the hips but, because of the strength required, there is a tendency to move them sideways before returning to the centre line – this gives the feathering movement which is sometimes seen. Constant propulsion cannot be obtained from the arms for once the pulling part of the arm action is completed there must be a pause in propulsion until the arms have recovered to start their pulling action again.

Breathing. As the arms are pulled down in the water the head is lifted until the mouth is just clear of the water and this is when a deep breath is taken. The face is submerged in the water with the breath held. As the arms are recovered to the forward position the air is forcibly exhaled into the water and the cycle is completed. This is termed the explosive method of breathing and is the most effective in this stroke. As the swimmer becomes more efficient alternate breathing may be practised i.e. breath is inhaled at every other stroke cycle. Some swimmers find it easier to breathe to the side as in the crawl stroke – this does help body position and increases speed. However care must be taken that the shoulders remain in the horizontal position to conform to the laws laid down for this stroke.

Timing. There may be variations in the timing depending on the physical structure of the swimmer but it is usual to have two leg beats to one complete arm cycle of the stroke. The first leg beat is made as the hands just start to pull down and the second one starts just prior to the recovery of the arms. The rhythm of the stroke can be heard as the feet beat the water and a continuous and fast leg action can be produced and the arm movement seems to fit into this rhythm quite naturally.

Practices. It is usual to introduce this stroke as a follow-on from the breast stroke from which it has evolved. As in the other strokes it should be introduced by a visual demonstration either on film or in the water. It is better to teach it as a whole stroke starting with 2 breast stroke leg kicks to 1 butterfly arm stroke. This helps to slow down the movement by using the glide and this is most important. Practice should be limited at the beginning. The next stage is a demonstration of the dolphin kick. Practise at the side of the bath flapping the feet down on to the water. Emphasize the beat of the feet and then progress by increasing the speed of the movement with the legs not going so deeply into the water. Continue this practice using a float and then with arms extended above the head.

The arm action should be practised first from the standing position with shoulders at water level and then it should be combined with breathing from the same position. From the glide use arms only allowing legs to trail.

The full stroke practice then follows with a glide from the side and using three dolphin kicks to one arm action. Again limit the practice to not more than two complete cycles. The strenuous nature of this stroke calls for very limited practices at all stages. As proficiency is achieved the number of leg beats may be reduced to 2 per cycle, alternate breathing introduced and side breathing tried.

The English Back Stroke

This is now an 'old-fashioned' stroke with no place at all in competitive swimming and rarely mentioned in books on swimming. There are other aspects to swimming than competitive swimming and, I feel, more important ones. Because of the very high standard of competitive swimming at all levels today the 'life' of the competitive swimmer is limited to a maximum of fifteen years – there are exceptions but not many. There are those who have swum for sixty years or more for recreation and most of us learn to swim in the first instance as a means of survival.

If nothing else, the ability to swim the English Back Stroke is the acquiring of a skill and, without the use of the arms, it is one of the most valuable strokes used in life-saving and for this reason alone it should be taught.

Body position. The body position for the back glide, learnt when practising the back crawl, is the same for the English Back Stroke. The head is raised sufficiently to be able to look at the toes without any undue strain of the neck muscles.

Leg action. The legs are bent from the knees and as they do this the knees open sideways almost as wide as they will go. The toes are pointed downwards and outwards and the legs are swung in an outward and circular movement from the knees. They are then brought together in line with the body with the ankles stretched. The thrust comes from the insteps and the front of the legs being pushed against the water. At the completion of the stroke there is a glide and the whole action is a smooth and continuous one.

Arm action. In the life-saving stroke there is no arm action although the leg action is the same as for the English Back Stroke. In the latter the arms are raised over the head with the wrists turning so that the hands are back to back. The hands meet over the head and there is a pause. The arms are then turned so that the palms are vertical then sweep them round and back to the sides keeping the elbows straight.

Breathing. As the arms recover by their backwards swing over the head you inhale through the mouth and exhale after the pause when the arms come down to the sides.

Timing. From the starting position with the arms extended above the head with the backs of the hands turned inward and touching the arms are pulled sideways and downwards to the outside of the legs and at the same time breathing out. This is followed by the glide (but not in the life-saving stroke) and as you make the leg kick the arms return to the starting position and you inhale through the mouth.

Practices. The arm action can be practised with the toes under the rail or with a float between the knees. The leg action can be practised with first arms by the sides, with possibly a small sculling movement of the hands, and then with arms stretched over the head. Previous practices for the back crawl will have helped.

The Side Stroke
A very brief mention of a stroke which is still of value for it is the least energetic of all strokes and can be kept up for long distances. It is of great value in life-saving for towing and with the rescuer's face sideways it allows regular breathing. To describe it briefly – it is the breast stroke swum on the side with the face resting on the water with the upper arm providing propulsion by doing the crawl arm action and doing a scissor kick with the legs!

Conclusion
I hope that the foregoing notes will prove of some value to the teacher of swimming. They are brief and very general and are given as a guide for teaching beginners and not for those who wish to take part in competitive swimming of a high standard.

All coaches are teachers but not all teachers are coaches although they do lay the foundations on which the coaches work. As teachers of swimming we have to sell our subject and gain the interest of the children, we have to teach beginners in large numbers and we have to teach for recreation and survival. The coach, on the other hand, deals mainly with individuals who wish to take part in competitive and speed swimming, who desire to improve and to pit their strengths against others and who are willing to do a lot of very hard work to achieve their ends.

Chapter 8: Water Safety

Over 300 children drowned in one year in England and Wales! What a terrible tragedy – so many young lives lost and so many families bereaved. Yet most of these children's lives would have been saved had they been able to swim only a short distance.

How can we help to reduce this appalling and unnecessary loss of life? The first and most important way is by doing all we can to teach every child to swim. The second way, and also very important, is to make children aware of the potential dangers in the water and on the water and to teach them simple rules of behaviour when near the water and what to do in an emergency

The Royal Society for the Prevention of Accidents, through its Water Safety Organizer, is only too happy to help schools with advice, posters and handbooks on Water Safety. Schools themselves can help the children by giving talks on Water Safety and by showing films and other visual aids.

The following simple rules of Water Safety are, or should be, well-known but I make no apology for repeating them here as I feel that they are so very important to us all.

1. Learn to swim.
2. Never swim alone. There is safety in numbers.
3. Obey danger signals. The red flag means No Swimming.
4. Avoid taking risks. Not only do you endanger your own life but you may endanger the lives of others.
5. Avoid bathing near obstacles such as rocks, piers, wrecks which can cause currents.
6. Never use rubber toys, air beds etc. in open waters.
7. Do not swim after balls carried out to sea.
8. Swim in line with the shore or river bank and keep within your own depth.
9. Even if you are a strong swimmer never swim out to sea unless you are accompanied by a boat.

10. Do not bathe after a heavy meal or when you are not feeling well.
11. Do not stay in the water if you are feeling cold.
12. Avoid horseplay in or near water. An unexpected or accidental blow could cause concussion and perhaps drowning.
13. Avoid diving until you are sure that the water is deep enough and that there are no hidden obstacles.
14. Never give a false alarm. You may endanger someone else's life.
15. Avoid swimming in rivers where there are weeds – you might get entangled.
16. Beware of big waves – learn to dive through them.
17. Avoid sandbanks and caves – you might get cut-off by the tide.
18. Never go swimming without permission.
19. Learn life-saving and how to give artificial respiration.
20. Even if you cannot swim find out what to do in an emergency. Study for and take the Water Safety Award of the Royal Life Saving Society – it is for inexperienced and non-swimmers.

And for Parents

1. Learn to swim – you never know when it can help.
2. Learn elementary resuscitation.
3. Supervise children playing near water of any kind.
4. Protect ornamental pools in the garden with wire netting.
5. Cover water butts and tanks when not in use.
6. If you live near gravel pits, rivers, canals or ponds make sure that your fences and hedges are in good repair so that young children cannot stray.
7. Do not allow your children to use airbeds or rubber rings on open waters unless they are secured by lines to a fixed point and then only if the children are under adult supervision.
8. When in charge of a group of children keep a constant and careful check of them when they are in the water and do not swim yourself.
9. Never allow children to bathe when the red danger flag is flying or near any notice warning you that it is dangerous to bathe.
10. Many children who go fishing alone are drowned through slipping into the water from perhaps a deep bank. Heavy clothes and rubber boots may weigh them down and they are unable to clamber out. Never let your children go fishing alone.

11. If you are fond of boating and yachting make sure that every child wears a life jacket and that the younger ones are attached to a line.

12. Never take a boat out unless you are experienced in its use and you have checked the weather and the tides with the local authority.

Chapter 9: Omissions

There are several aspects of swimming which I might have dealt with but which I have omitted for various reasons and I would just like to mention these.

Diving
I have written the preceding chapters with teaching swimming baths uppermost in my mind and these will rarely exceed 4 feet in depth. This depth of water is not sufficient for one to teach even the simplest of dives although the introduction to diving may be taught in almost any water. This introduction would consist of exercises to encourage the child to swim under water with eyes open and to dive from the surface either from the standing or glide position. I would not go beyond that in a shallow bath.

The very minimum depth of water into which any head-first entry should be made is at least the height of the diver plus arms stretched above the head. A six-foot tall boy making a vertical entry into the water would require a depth of at least nine feet. Not only height but weight is also a consideration for a falling body has momentum in which weight is an important factor. Many of you will remember, and probably still use today, the baths built in the early part of the century where, from fixed boards of varying height people used to dive into not more than six feet of water. Most authorities have now removed all these boards because of the great danger of serious accident. The Amateur Swimming Association has laid it down that the *minimum* depth of water for any form of competitive diving or practice is 9 feet 10 inches (3 metres) and all new baths with diving facilities comply with this.

Diving today is a streamlined scientific sport. It should be taught by experts and should be written about by experts, and I am no expert.

Synchronized Swimming
The term Synchronized Swimming is applied to any form of aquatic

movement by one or more performers synchronized to a musical accompaniment and/or to each other. To me this form of swimming seems to have evolved from the fancy or trick swimming displayed at swimming galas as an attraction in the interval some thirty or forty years ago. It might be described as a form of water ballet and is a most attractive spectacle. One thinks of it as a pastime for girls but I do not think that there are any rules forbidding it for boys.

Many girls who have learnt to swim quite well but who have no desire to take part in competitive swimming have found this synchronized swimming a very worthwhile activity. The various water skills required have a considerable value in themselves for their performance requires muscular co-ordination and control and is a challenge to creativeness and imagination. The accomplishment of the various skills and the all-round exercise obtained together with the training for survival ability gained through watermanship make it an ideal addition to the Physical Education programme.

A knowledge of all strokes, including side stroke, is required but the strokes are swum for effect rather than speed. The basic skills may be introduced into the teaching of swimming in Primary Schools as a change of activity and to improve ability in the water. Two awards for synchronized swimming have been introduced by the Swimming Teachers Association and George W. Rackham has written an excellent book, published by Faber, on the subject.

Water Polo

Water Polo is a game which can be played by boys and men who are competent swimmers but the great difficulty is finding the right facilities and enough available bath time for it to be played. Each team consists of seven players and four reserves who can be interchanged throughout the game. Most swimming clubs have a water polo team and the rules are governed by the A.S.A.

It is a game which was introduced by this country nearly a hundred years ago. There are local leagues and County and National Championships and it has a world-wide popularity. It was introduced into the Olympic Games in 1900.

Swimming for the Physically Handicapped Children

It is agreed that swimming is the finest physical activity for physically handicapped children. The therapeutic value, both physical and psychological, is great for although these children delight in movement e.g. to music where their movements though rhythmical are restricted, such movement is not easy on land and it is only in the water that they become far more mobile and can more easily do exercises which help them to build up their muscle strength.

The teaching of these children must be done in the first instance on an individual basis and there must be helpers with the children in the water. Many members of swimming clubs give tremendous help in this way. The teacher or therapist must understand each individual case and know how the water can be used to assist movement.

Although the teaching of swimming to the handicapped is a job for the experienced and trained teacher or therapist there are many of our practices for beginners which can be used in a modified form. May I refer you to the book *Teaching the Physically Handicapped to Swim* (Anderson) published by Faber.

Organization of a Swimming Gala

At one time school and district swimming galas were almost social events. There was a lot of fun and enjoyment for the children and there was participation by not only all the teachers but by the majority of the children. Even those children who could not swim found that there was some activity at the shallow end in which they could take part. The announcer was the person with the loudest voice (there were no loud speakers) and the judges were kind friends who could be enticed to help. At the end of the gala everyone, swimmers, officials and guests were entertained to free Bovril kindly contributed by the makers.

But those happy days are gone. Today our galas, even at school level, are highly organized affairs with the officials all properly qualified at the correct level, with events based on the four major strokes of standards undreamt of not many years ago, with certified stop-watches correct to one-tenth of a second trained on each child and with a tenseness formerly found only at National and International Events.

May I make one plea that in our school galas at least let us have some fun and as many as possible of the children taking part even if it is only an egg and spoon race in the shallow end or being knocked off a greasy pole! By all means have speed races for the better swimmers but let us not forget less able children.

I could produce an efficient 'blue print' for the organization of a swimming gala but this has been done in many books and space does not permit here. Commonsense and some experience are the greatest assets in organizing a successful school gala.

Appendix A: List of Addresses

The following list of addresses may be of some value.

English Schools Swimming Association (for general information on swimming with particular reference to swimming activities in schools).
Hon. Secretary: Mr E. H. Burden, 190 Nether Street, London, N.3.

Teaching Swimming Bath Scheme of the English Schools Swimming Association (for general information on the provision of school swimming baths).
Hon. Secretary: Mr J. H. Warrick, 47 Woodhall Gate, Pinner, Middlesex.
Hon. Treasurer: Mr F. J. E. Rudge, 159 Herkomes Road, Bushey, Herts, WD2 3LH.

Amateur Swimming Association (for general information on all swimming activities, training courses, films, etc.).
Hon. Secretary: Harold Fern House, Derby Square, Loughborough, Leicester.
For information on all the awards of the A.S.A. and the Joint A.S.A., E.S.S.A. schemes please write to The Organizer, Miss L. V. Cook, 12 Kings Avenue, Woodford Green, Essex.

The Royal Life Saving Society (for all information on life-saving, resuscitation, awards, films etc.).
The Secretary: Desborough House, 14 Devonshire Street, Portland Place, London, W.1.

The Royal Society for the Prevention of Accidents (for information on all aspects of Water Safety, Posters, Handbooks, Learn to Swim Campaigns, etc.).
The Water Safety Organizer, RoSPA, Royal Oak Centre, Brighton Road, Purley, Surrey, CR2 2UR.

The Swimming Teachers Association (for details of examinations, courses, etc.).
National Secretary: R. Clements Esq., Queen's College Chambers, 38A Paradise Street, Birmingham 1.

The Surf Life Saving Association of Great Britain (for information on the activities of the Association, hire of films etc.).
The Secretary, 4 Cathedral Yard, Exeter, Devon.

The British Red Cross Society (for information on resuscitation etc.). 14/15 Grosvenor Crescent, London, S.W.1.

The St. John Ambulance Association (for information on resuscitation etc.). 1 Grosvenor Crescent, London, S.W.1.

The Central Council of Physical Recreation (for general water activities, adults' and children's courses, etc.).
The Secretary, 26/29 Park Crescent, London, W.1.

The Royal National Lifeboat Institution (for films etc. on rescue at sea). 42 Grosvenor Gardens, London, S.W.1.

(The addresses of the branches of the above Associations in Ireland, Scotland and Wales may be obtained through the above.)

The Physical Education Association of Great Britain and Northern Ireland (for general information and their journal). Ling House, 10 Nottingham Place, London, W.1.

Association of Swimming Pool Contractors (experts on all aspects of swimming pool construction. Information sheets on Design, Construction, Filtration and Heating of swimming pools). List of members of the Association and copies of the information sheets obtainable from The Secretary, 61-63 Holywell Road, Watford, Herts.

The Swimming Pool Review (Quarterly journal dealing with every aspect of swimming pools. 80p per annum post free). Published by Clarke & Hunter (London) Ltd., Armour House, Bridge Street, Guildford, Surrey.

The Swimming Times (Monthly magazine of interest to all teachers and swimmers. 10p per month. By post £1·50 per annum). Obtainable from The Swimming Times, Harold Fern House, Derby Square, Loughborough, Leics.

Bovril Ltd (for swimming charts and leaflets). Bovril House, Southbury Road, Enfield, Middlesex.

Perkins Engines Ltd (Water Safety Film). Film Library, Perkins Engines Ltd, Peterborough.

British Film Institute (Full list of films on water activities). Booking Manager, Distribution Department, British Film Institute, 42-43 Lower Marsh Lane, London, S.E.1.

Appendix B: Books on Swimming

The following list of books on swimming and allied sports may prove of value. It is not for me to recommend any one of them – I have read at some time practically all of them – and from each one have gained something. Publishers are very willing to send you inspection copies and County Librarians might be persuaded to hold copies of them all. The ideal place for the books of your choice is, of course, in your school's reference library. One or two of the books may now be out of print. There are three books which I feel every school should have and these are:

The Teaching of Swimming, an official handbook of the Amateur Swimming Association, and published by Educational Productions Ltd.

Swimming and Diving, the official book of swimming of the English Schools' Swimming Association, and published by William Heinemann (new edition).

Life Saving and Water Safety, the official handbook of the Royal Life Saving Society, published by the Society.

Book List
Official publications of the A.S.A. (obtainable from the Hon. Secretary):

The Teaching of Swimming, Educational Productions Ltd.
Swimming and Swimming Strokes, Educational Productions Ltd.
Diving Instructions, Educational Productions Ltd.
Diving Manual, Educational Productions Ltd.
Competitive Swimming, Educational Productions Ltd.
Survival Swimming, Educational Productions Ltd.
Swimming, Educational Productions Ltd.
Better Swimming, Educational Productions Ltd.
Swimming to Win, Educational Productions Ltd.

Swimming for Schools, A. H. Owen, Pelham Books Ltd.
Swimming to Win – For All Ages, Don Talbot, Pelham Books Ltd.
Forbes Carlile on Swimming, Forbes Carlile, Pelham Books Ltd.
Diving for Teacher and Pupil, R. M. Dawson, Pelham Books Ltd.
The Science of Swimming, J. Counsilman, Pelham Books Ltd.
Dryland Exercises for Swimmers, Buck Dawson, Pelham Books Ltd.
Swimming, R. J. Kiphuth, Nicholas Kaye.
Basic Swimming, Kiphuth and Burke, Nicholas Kaye.
Swimming and Diving, D. A. Armbruster and L. E. Morehouse, Nicholas Kaye.
Springboard Diving, P. Moriarty, Nicholas Kaye.
How to Swim Well, Charles Sava, Hodder & Stoughton.
Sports Illustrated Book of Swimming, Matt Mann, Hodder & Stoughton.
Swimming for Teachers and Youth Leaders, M. A. Jarvis, Faber.
Your Book of Swimming, M. A. Jarvis, Faber.
Your Book of Diving, M. A. Jarvis, Faber.
Your Book of Survival Swimming, M. A. Jarvis, Faber.
Teaching the Physically Handicapped to Swim, William Anderson, Faber.
Learning to Swim, H. Littlewood, G. Bell & Sons.
Let's All Go Swimming, Reg Laxton, Stanley Paul.
Swimming, Bill Juba, Stanley Paul.
Instructions to Young Swimmers, Bill Juba, Museum Press.
Swimming, J. G. Garstang, Museum Press.
Teaching Children to Swim, Istvan Barany, Collets.
Teach Yourself Swimming, Frank Waterman, English University Press.
Boys and Girls Swim Book, Sid Hedges, Methuen.
Crawl and Butterfly Swimming, Sid Hedges, Methuen.
Swimming is for Everyone, Sid Hedges, Methuen.
The Shallow Water Method, Winifred Gibson, Pitman.
To Start you Crawling, Winifred Gibson, Pitman.
Learn to Swim the Crawl, H. Olsson, Pitman.
Water Babe, Judy Grinham, Oldbourne Book Co.
Teach Your Child to Swim, Edna Sims, Pearson.
Get Swimming, Howard and Grainge, Souvenir Press.
Better Swimming for Boys and Girls, H. Elkington and A. Holmyard, Kaye & Ward.
First Strokes in Swimming, Forsberg, Routledge & Kegan Paul.
Swimming, George Rackham, Collins.

Swimming for Schoolboys, F. L. Briscoe, Pelham Books.
Swimming and Water Sports, J. Edmundson, Pan Books.
Teaching an Infant to Swim, Virginia Newman, Angus & Robertson.

Life Saving
Life Saving and Water Safety, Royal Life Saving Society.
Life Saving (Know the Game Series), Educational Productions Ltd.

Underwater Swimming
Dive – The Complete Book of Skin Diving, Carrier, Nicholas Kaye.
Underwater Swimming, Leo Zandli, English University Press.
Diving Manual, Brooks and Broadhurst, Macdonald & Co.
Snorkel Diver, Matkin and Brooks, Macdonald & Co.
Scuba Diving, Van Ellman, Thomas Nelson.

Surfing
How to Surf, M. Farrelly and C. McGregor, Sphere Books Ltd.
Surfing, H. A. Kleine, Kaye & Ward.
Better Surfing, Cook and Romeika, Kaye & Ward.

Water Ski-ing
Water Ski-ing, Dick Pope, Nicholas Kaye.
Master Water Ski-ing, Maurois and Vazeille, Souvenir Press.
Water-Ski-ing, Ralph Hester, Pelham Books Ltd.

Land Conditioning
Circuit Training, Morgan and Anderson, G. Bell & Sons.
How to be Fit, R. J. H. Kiphuth, Nicholas Kaye.
Weight Training, Michael Fallon, Nicholas Kaye.

Periodicals
E.S.S.A. Handbook. Published annually. Contains reports of the work of the Association, Results of Competitions, Standard Times, Conditions of Awards etc. and is invaluable for teachers of swimming. (From Hon. Sec.)
A.S.A. Handbook. Published annually in April. (From Hon. Sec.)
The Swimming Times. Published monthly. A magazine of interest to

teachers and swimmers. Been published for 48 years, has over 20,000 readers and is read in 60 countries. From Editor, Capt. Bert Cummins.

The Swimming Pool Review. Published quarterly. Contains a wealth of information for those interested in swimming baths.

Appendix C: Wall Charts, Pamphlets, Posters

Wall Charts
A.S.A. Wall Charts available from Bovril Ltd., Bovril House, Southbury Road, Enfield, Middlesex.
(a) Swimming. Set of five.
(b) Diving. Set of five.
(c) Survival Swimming. Set of three.
(d) Competitive Swimming. Set of five.

Swimming Charts. Educational Productions Ltd., East Ardsley, Wakefield, Yorks. Three charts on Breast Stroke, Front Crawl and Back Crawl. Published in collaboration with the A.S.A. 20" × 30".

Rescue and Resuscitation Chart. Royal Life Saving Society.

First Aid Treatment in the Home. St. John's Ambulance Association. 8" × 8". Includes expired air and cardiac massage methods.

Pamphlets
Learning to swim and dive. Available free in any quantity from Bovril Ltd.

Snorkel Mask and Flipper Swimming. Available free from Phillips, Scott and Turner Co. Ltd., St Marks Hill, Surbiton, Surrey.

On the Water In the Water. RoSPA.

The Water Sports Code. Available free from Central Council of Physical Recreation.

Learn Water Sense. Children 6–11. RoSPA.

Learn the Water Safety Rules. Children 6–11. RoSPA.

Posters
RoSPA has a variety of posters, wall charts, Water Safety Packs. Please apply for full list. Prices are reduced for bulk orders. Your local education authority should be supplying you with these.

Appendix D: Swimming Films, Film Strips and Loops.

The following letters after the title of the film indicate from whom the film may be borrowed. Details of hire or films should be obtained from hirer (addresses in Appendix A). All films are 16 mm.

- A. AMATEUR SWIMMING ASSOCIATION.
- Ro. ROYAL SOCIETY FOR THE PREVENTION OF ACCIDENTS.
- RL. ROYAL LIFE SAVING SOCIETY.
- SL. SURF LIFE SAVING SOCIETY.
- RN. ROYAL NATIONAL LIFEBOAT INSTITUTION.
- B. BRITISH FILM INSTITUTE.
- P. PERKINS ENGINES LTD.
- PG. PGL ADVENTURE FILMS.

Getting Used to the Water (A). Sound. 12½ mins. Full teaching notes. Confidence exercises, correct breathing, gliding, leg kick, strokes.

Starting to Swim (A). Sound. 12½ mins. Early training. Exercises by class of 10-year-olds. Preparation for swimming strokes. Teaching notes.

Breast Stroke (A). Sound. 17 mins. Teaching notes. Demonstrated by International. Class introduced to stroke. Practices shown.

Learning the Front Crawl (A). Sound. 15 mins. Notes as above. (Breast).

Learning the Back Crawl (A). Sound. 12½ mins. Notes as above. (Breast).

Learning the Butterfly Stroke (A). Sound. 11 mins. Notes as above. (Breast).

Survival Swimming (A). Sound. 14½ mins. Shots of actual survival situation. Skills demonstrated in detail. Teaching notes.

Starting Synchronized Swimming (A). Sound. 17 mins. Shows basic skills, followed by demonstration and team sequence.

Learning to Swim with Artificial Aids (A). 11 mins. Shows various aids and uses. Multi-stroke method using aids.

Starting to Dive (A). Sound. 10 mins. Class of children being taken through confidence practices leading to plunge diver, plain header and diving for fun.

APPENDIX

Springboard Diving (A). Sound. 13½ mins. Introduces springboard diving to a class of children. Some trampoline training. Demonstrations.

I'm No Fool in Water (Ro). Sound. Colour. 9 mins. Walt Disney. Shows dangers present when swimming or playing in water.

Sensibly to Sea (Ro). Sound. Colour. 13 mins. The first cruise in small sailing cruiser showing essential safety points.

Survival Swimming (Ro). Sound. Colour. 11 mins. Lesson with primary school children in teaching pool in Plymouth.

Water Safety (Ro). Sound. Colour. 28 mins. Shows factors affecting safety of young children and adults when swimming, boating etc. Free loan from Sound Services Ltd., Kingston Road, London, S.W. 19.

Emergency Resuscitation (RL). Sound. Colour. Part 1. *Breathing for others*. 14 mins. Shows use of expired air method in many situations. Part 2. *Seconds Count*. 15 mins. Incidents where expired air method may be quickest way of saving life. Part 3. *Close Chest Cardiac Massage*. Demonstrates techniques of this method. 12 mins.

To Match Your Courage (RL). Sound. Colour. 22 mins. Shows work of Royal Life Saving Society.

Champions of the Surf (SL). Sound. Colour. 25 minutes. Shows work of Surf Life Saving Association of Great Britain.

That They May Live. A Gateway Film. Colour. Sound. 30 mins. Mouth to Mouth Resuscitation. Most impressive. Obtainable through Educational Foundation for Visual Aids.

A Rocket for Charlie (P). Sound. Colour. 13 mins. Two men take families boating with outboard motor. One does everything correctly and the other the opposite and brings family to near tragedy. Free.

Speed for Safety (RN). Sound. Colour. 15 mins. Shows typical rescues by inshore rescue boats of R.N.L.I. Free loan.

Lifeboat Call (RN). Sound. Colour. 11½ mins. The day's work of a lifeboat crew with eventually two boys being rescued. Free loan.

Every Second Counts (RN). Sound. Colour. 16 mins. Drifting airbeds, swimmer too far out to sea, etc. all calls on life-boat. Free loan.

Canoeing – The Basic Skills (B). Sound. Colour. 23 mins. Demonstration by experts of the principles of canoeing.

Film Loops
Film loops have to be purchased. Most of the loops are in slow motion to aid study of techniques shown. Most are 16 mm but some are 8 mm.

Swimming 1967. Series of 16 loops, 4 each on Front Crawl, Butterfly, Back Stroke and Breast Stroke. From A.S.A. or Educational Productions.

Synchronized Swimming (A). 16 mm. Series of 6 loops demonstrating basic skills of synchronized swimming.

Bruce Harlan Loops (A). *Swimming.* 18 loops showing world's leading swimmers on four strokes. *Diving.* 27 loops showing sixty different styles by world's greatest divers.

Diving. 12 loops showing diving movements and actions for coaching, Educational Productions.

Emergency Resuscitation. 3 8 mm. colour film loops of Mouth-to-Mouth, Mouth-to-Nose and External Cardiac Massage prepared in conjunction with Guy's Hospital, obtainable from Macmillan & Co.

Film Strips

The number of film strips on swimming and allied sports is very limited. E.F.V.A., Common Ground and Hulton had series of them but as they were made some 20 years ago they are now very dated.

The Royal Life Saving Society has three strips available, 'Instructional Drill for the Expired Air Method of Artificial Respiration', 'Releases from a Clutch' and 'Rescues from Drowning'. Details may be obtained from the Society.

St. John Ambulance Association have a film strip on 'Respiratory Resuscitation' with 16 frames.

Appendix E: Swimming Awards

Many children thrive on the incentives provided by swimming awards which give them the encouragement to improve their swimming both in ability and variety. The life-saving and survival awards help them to become more competent and responsible citizens.

Probably the most treasured award given to any child is the first certificate he receives from his school for swimming even if it is only for one width for this is the first great step. I do suggest that all schools get a simple certificate printed for issue to their own children for the first stages.

Many local education authorities have their own range of swimming certificates and so do some Schools' Swimming Associations. The following lists of awards may be of some help. Full details may be obtained from the Associations concerned (see list in Appendix A).

Amateur Swimming Association/English Schools' Swimming Association
Joint Awards Scheme.
(*a*) Incentive Awards.
    (i) 25 yards certificate.
    (ii) 50 yards certificate (with jump or head-first entry).
    (iii) 100 yards certificate (with jump or head-first entry).
    Certificates for these awards are supplied in bulk to the Education Authority or in 50s to individual schools.
(*b*) Proficiency Awards.
    Stage 1.
    Stage 2.
(*c*) Speed Swimming Awards.
    (i) Merit Award.
    (ii) Advanced Award.
(*d*) Awards for the Physically Handicapped.
    (i) Preliminary.
    (ii) Intermediate.
    (iii) Advanced.

Amateur Swimming Association
Awards for Proficiency in Personal Survival.
(*a*) Bronze Award.
(*b*) Silver Award.
(*c*) Gold Award.

Royal Life Saving Society
(*a*) Water Safety Award. For inexperienced and non-swimmers to learn how to give simple basic help to someone in difficulty in the water.
(*b*) Safety Awards.
  (i) Preliminary.
  (ii) Advanced.
(*c*) Preliminary Resuscitation Award.
(*d*) Elementary Award.
(*e*) Intermediate Award.
(*f*) Other Awards such as Bronze Medallion, Award of Merit, etc. are of a more advanced nature and there is a downward age limit.

The Swimming Teachers' Association
(*a*) Endeavour Award.
(*b*) Junior Swimmer Award.
(*c*) Cadet Award.
(*d*) Complete Swimmer. Three Grades, Bronze, Silver and Gold.
(*e*) Synchro Primer – preparation for all synchronized swimming activities.
(*f*) Synchro Swimmer.

Other Awards
Other awards are issued by
> Scottish and Welsh A.S.A.
> The Scout Association.
> The Girl Guides Association.
> The Boys' Brigade.
> The Girls' Brigade.

Note: Some Education Authorities pay entrance fees for some of the above Awards. Please make inquiries from your Education Officer or P.E. Organizer.